Money-Saving Mastery

Strategies for Financial Success

Luna Z. Rainstorm

Xspurts.com

A New Zealand Designed Product

Other Versions Available

Why limit yourself to just one format?

This book is now available in physical, digital, and audiobook options.

Choose the way you love to read and dive into the story today. You won't regret it!

Digital ISBN: 9781776968817
Physical ISBN: 9781776968800
Audio ISBN:

To obtain a different format of this book at a discounted price, please get in touch with us at:

http://isbn.xspurts.com/

Contents

Have Questions / Comments?

This book was designed to cover as much information as possible, but I know I have probably missed something, or some new amazing discovery has just come out.

If you notice something missing or have a question that I failed to answer, please get in touch and let me know. If I can, I will email you an answer and also update the book so others can also benefit from it.

Thanks For Being Awesome :)

Submit Your Questions / Comments At:

https://questions.xspurts.com

Get Free Stuff

We love writing and have produced a huge number of books.

For being one of our amazing readers, we would love to offer you more books we have created, 100% free.

To claim this limited time special offer, simply go to the site below and enter your name and email address.

You will then receive loads (as we love our readers so much :) of our great books, content and audio direct to your email account, 100% free!

Get Loads of FREE Stuff at:

https://free.xspurts.com

Chapter One

The Psychology of Saving Money

Saving money is a common goal that many people have, yet it can be challenging to achieve. One of the reasons why saving money can be difficult is due to the psychology behind it. Understanding the psychological factors that influence our saving habits can help us make better decisions and increase our chances of achieving our financial goals.

One psychological factor that affects our saving habits is the concept of delayed gratification. Delayed gratification is the ability to resist the temptation of immediate rewards in favor of long-term benefits. In the context of saving money, this means that we have to forgo immediate pleasures, such as buying a new gadget or going on a luxurious vacation, in order to save for our future needs, such as retirement or emergency expenses.

Studies have shown that people who are better at delaying gratification tend to be more successful in achieving their financial goals. This is because they are more willing to make sacrifices in the short-term for the sake of long-term gains. However, not everyone is naturally good at delaying gratification. Some people may have a stronger inclination towards instant gratification, which can make it harder for them to save money.

Another psychological factor that affects our saving habits is our level of self-control. Self-control refers to our ability to regulate our thoughts, emotions, and behaviors in order to achieve a goal. In the context of saving money, self-control means that we have to resist the temptation to spend money on unnecessary things and instead prioritize our financial goals.

Research has shown that self-control is a limited resource that can become depleted over time. This means that if we are constantly resisting temptations throughout the day, our ability to control our impulses may weaken, making it more likely for us to give in to the temptation to spend money. Therefore, it is important to be mindful of our self-control levels and to plan our spending and saving habits accordingly.

Another psychological factor that influences our saving habits is our level of financial literacy. Financial literacy refers to our knowledge and understanding of financial concepts and principles, such as budgeting, saving, investing, and debt management. People who are more financially literate tend to make better financial decisions and are more likely to save money.

However, many people lack basic financial literacy skills. This can make it difficult for them to understand the importance of saving and to make informed decisions about their finances. Therefore, it is important to invest in financial education and to seek out resources and information that can help us improve our financial literacy skills.

In addition to these psychological factors, there are also social and cultural factors that influence our saving habits. For example, our social networks and cultural norms can shape our attitudes and beliefs about money and saving. If our friends and family members have a culture of spending and little emphasis on saving, we may be more likely to adopt similar behaviors.

Similarly, our cultural values and beliefs about money can also influence our saving habits. For example, in some cultures, there may be a greater emphasis on saving and frugality as a means of achieving financial stability and security. In other cultures, spending and consumption may be seen as a way of demonstrating social status and success.

In conclusion, the psychology of saving money is complex and multifaceted. Understanding the psychological factors that influence our saving habits can help us make better financial decisions and increase our chances of achieving our financial goals. By being mindful of our tendencies towards instant gratification, monitoring our self-control levels, investing in our financial literacy, and being aware of the social and cultural factors that shape our attitudes towards money, we can develop healthier saving habits that will benefit us in the long run.

Understanding Your Money Mindset

Money is an essential part of our lives, yet many of us struggle to manage it effectively. One of the reasons why we may find it difficult to save money is due to our money mindset. Our money mindset refers to the beliefs, attitudes, and values we hold about money, and how these shape our behaviors and decisions regarding money.

Understanding your money mindset can be a powerful tool in helping you achieve your financial goals. By becoming aware of your beliefs and attitudes towards money, you can identify any limiting beliefs or negative thought patterns that may be holding you back from achieving financial success.

One common money mindset that can make it difficult to save money is a scarcity mindset. A scarcity mindset is a belief that there is a limited amount of money or resources available, and that one must compete or struggle to secure their share. This mindset can lead to a fear of not having enough money, which can result in overspending or hoarding money.

On the other hand, an abundance mindset is a belief that there is an unlimited supply of money and resources available, and that one can create wealth and prosperity through hard work and creativity. People with an abundance mindset tend to have a more positive attitude towards money and are more likely to save and invest their money wisely.

Another common money mindset that can make it difficult to save money is a poverty mindset. A poverty mindset is a belief that money is evil, corrupt, or unnecessary, and that people who have money are greedy or selfish. This mindset can lead to a lack of motivation or interest in managing one's finances and can result in financial struggles.

Conversely, a wealth mindset is a belief that money is a tool for creating opportunities, achieving goals, and making a positive impact in the world. People with a wealth mindset tend to view money as a resource to be used wisely and strategically, and are more likely to save and invest their money for future goals.

Another money mindset that can impact our saving habits is a belief in instant gratification. Instant gratification refers to the desire for immediate pleasure or reward, even at the expense of long-term goals or consequences. People who prioritize instant gratification over long-term goals may find it difficult to save money or make responsible financial decisions.

In contrast, people who prioritize delayed gratification are more likely to save money and make wise financial decisions. Delayed gratification involves sacrificing immediate pleasure for the sake of long-term benefits, such as saving money for retirement or investing in education or business ventures.

One way to understand your money mindset is to examine your attitudes and behaviors towards money. Ask yourself questions such as:

What do I believe about money? Is money evil, or a tool for creating opportunities and achieving goals?

Do I prioritize immediate gratification, or am I willing to delay gratification for long-term benefits?

Do I have a scarcity mindset or an abundance mindset when it comes to money?

Am I afraid of not having enough money, or am I confident in my ability to create wealth and prosperity?

By examining your money mindset and identifying any limiting beliefs or negative thought patterns, you can begin to shift your attitudes and behaviors towards money in a more positive direction. This can involve adopting new beliefs and values that support your financial goals, such as a belief in abundance or delayed gratification, and letting go of any beliefs that may be holding you back, such as a belief in scarcity or poverty.

In addition to examining your money mindset, there are several practical steps you can take to improve your saving habits. These include:

1. Creating a budget: A budget can help you track your expenses and identify areas where you can cut back on spending and save more money.

2. Setting financial goals: Setting specific, measurable goals can help you stay motivated and focused on your saving and investing objectives.

3. Automating your savings: Setting up automatic payments so a set amount goes into a different account each week.

Creating a Positive Attitude Towards Saving

Saving money is an important part of financial planning, yet it can be challenging to maintain a positive attitude towards saving. Many people view saving as a sacrifice or a chore, rather than as a positive step towards achieving their financial goals. However, creating a positive attitude towards saving can help you stay motivated and committed to your financial objectives.

One way to create a positive attitude towards saving is to focus on the benefits of saving, rather than the sacrifices involved. Saving money can help you achieve your financial goals, such as buying a home, paying for education or starting a business. Saving can also provide a sense of security and peace of mind, knowing that you have a financial cushion to fall back on in case of emergencies.

Another way to create a positive attitude towards saving is to make it a fun and rewarding experience. Instead of viewing saving as a chore, try to make it a game or a challenge. For example, you could set a goal to save a certain amount of money each month, and reward yourself with a small treat or activity once you reach your goal. This can help you stay motivated and engaged in the process of saving.

It can also be helpful to develop a positive mindset towards money in general. Money is often viewed as a source of stress and anxiety, but it can also be a tool for achieving our goals and improving our lives. Developing a positive mindset towards money can help you feel more in control of your finances and confident in your ability to achieve your financial objectives.

Here are some practical steps you can take to develop a positive attitude towards saving:

1. Develop a clear financial plan: Setting specific, measurable goals can help you stay motivated and focused on your saving objectives. Make a list of your short-term and long-term financial goals, and develop a plan for achieving them. This could involve creating a budget, reducing expenses, and increasing your income through side hustles or part-time work.

2. Celebrate your successes: Saving money can be a long and challenging process, so it's important to celebrate your successes along the way. When you reach a savings milestone or achieve a financial goal, take the time

to acknowledge your accomplishments and reward yourself for your hard work.

3. Surround yourself with positive influences: The people you spend time with can have a big impact on your attitude towards money and saving. Surround yourself with people who have a positive mindset towards money and who support your financial goals. This could involve joining a savings group or online community, or seeking out a financial mentor or coach.

4. Practice gratitude: Gratitude is a powerful tool for cultivating a positive attitude towards life, including your finances. Take time each day to reflect on the things you are grateful for, including your financial situation. By focusing on the positive aspects of your finances, you can develop a more optimistic and positive attitude towards saving.

5. Make saving a priority: Saving money should be a priority in your financial plan, not an afterthought. Make saving a regular habit by setting up automatic transfers from your checking account to your savings account. This can help you stay on track with your savings goals and make saving a more automatic and effortless process.

In conclusion, creating a positive attitude towards saving can help you stay motivated and committed to your financial goals. By focusing on the benefits of saving, making it a fun and rewarding experience, developing a positive mindset towards money, and taking practical steps to prioritize saving in your financial plan, you can cultivate a more optimistic and proactive attitude towards saving.

Overcoming Common Barriers to Saving

Saving money is an important part of financial planning, yet many people struggle to save as much as they would like. There are several common barriers to saving that can make it difficult to maintain a consistent savings plan. Understanding these barriers and developing strategies to overcome them can help you achieve your financial goals.

1. Lack of a budget: One of the biggest barriers to saving is not having a budget. Without a budget, it can be difficult to track your expenses and identify areas where you can cut back in order to save more money. To overcome this barrier, create a budget that includes all of your expenses and income. Identify areas where you can reduce your expenses, such as eating out less often or canceling subscriptions you don't use. Use the money you save to increase your savings.

2. High expenses: High expenses can make it difficult to save, particularly if you are living paycheck to paycheck. To overcome this barrier, focus on reducing your expenses wherever possible. Look for ways to cut back on unnecessary expenses, such as dining out or buying luxury items. Consider downsizing your home or car, or finding ways to increase your income through side hustles or part-time work.

3. Debt: Debt can be a significant barrier to saving, particularly if you have high interest rates or large monthly payments. To overcome this barrier, focus on paying down your debt as quickly as possible. Consider consolidating your debt into a lower interest rate loan, or negotiating with your creditors to reduce your interest rates or monthly payments. Once you have paid off your debt, use the money you would have been paying towards debt to increase your savings.

4. Lack of motivation: Lack of motivation can make it difficult to maintain a consistent savings plan. To overcome this barrier, focus on the benefits of saving. Think about the financial goals you want to achieve, such as buying

a home or saving for retirement. Visualize yourself achieving these goals, and use this as motivation to stick to your savings plan.

5. Lack of accountability: Lack of accountability can make it easy to fall off track with your savings plan. To overcome this barrier, find an accountability partner who can help you stay motivated and on track. This could be a friend or family member who is also trying to save money, or a financial advisor who can provide guidance and support.

6. Lack of knowledge: Lack of knowledge about personal finance and investing can be a significant barrier to saving. To overcome this barrier, invest in your financial education. Read books and articles about personal finance and investing, take classes or workshops, and seek out the advice of financial professionals. The more you know about personal finance and investing, the better equipped you will be to make informed decisions about your money.

7. Lack of patience: Lack of patience can make it difficult to stick to a long-term savings plan. To overcome this barrier, focus on the long-term benefits of saving. Recognize that building wealth takes time, and that the benefits of saving will compound over time. Set small, achievable goals along the way to help you stay motivated and engaged in the process of saving.

In conclusion, overcoming common barriers to saving is an important part of achieving your financial goals. By creating a budget, reducing expenses, paying down debt, staying motivated and accountable, investing in your financial education, and cultivating patience, you can develop a consistent savings plan that will help you achieve your financial objectives.

The power of compounding interest.

The power of compounding interest is a financial concept that has long been celebrated for its ability to create wealth over time. By consistently saving and investing, individuals can take advantage of this powerful financial tool to build their assets over the long term.

At its core, compounding interest is the process of earning interest on both the principal amount and the interest that has already been earned. Essentially, it's the interest on interest, allowing your money to grow at an exponential rate. This is in contrast to simple interest, which only earns interest on the principal amount.

To illustrate the power of compounding interest, let's consider an example over a 25-year period with regular savings. Suppose you decide to invest $5,000 annually in an account with an average annual interest rate of 7%. At the end of the first year, you'll have earned $350 in interest ($5,000 x 0.07).

In the second year, you invest another $5,000, bringing the total amount invested to $10,000. The interest earned in the second year would be $735 ($10,000 x 0.07), as you're now earning interest on both the initial investment and the interest earned in the first year. As you continue to invest $5,000 each year, the interest will continue to compound, leading to substantial growth in your account balance.

After 25 years of consistently investing $5,000 annually and assuming a 7% interest rate, the total amount invested would be $125,000. However, due to the power of compounding interest, the final account balance would be a staggering $337,073.53.

This example highlights the significant impact of compounding interest over the long term. By consistently saving and allowing your interest to compound, you can create substantial wealth even with modest contributions.

It's important to note that the rate at which your investment grows is heavily influenced by the interest rate. In the example above, a 7% interest rate was used, but if the rate were lower, the final account balance would be considerably less. Conversely, if the rate were higher, the balance would be even more impressive.

Another key factor in maximizing the power of compounding interest is time. The longer your money has to grow, the more dramatic the effects of compounding will be. In the example above, the 25-year time frame allowed the investment to grow significantly. If the investment period were shorter, the growth would be less substantial, emphasizing the importance of starting early and staying consistent with your savings plan.

In summary, the power of compounding interest is a remarkable financial concept that allows individuals to build wealth over time. By understanding the principles of compounding interest and making a commitment to save and invest regularly, you can harness this powerful tool to create a financially secure future.

Chapter Two

Creating a Personalized Budget

Creating a personalized budget is a critical step towards achieving financial stability and saving money. A budget is a plan that outlines your income and expenses, and helps you track your spending and savings over time. A personalized budget takes into account your individual circumstances and financial goals, and provides a roadmap for achieving those goals.

Here are some steps to creating a personalized budget:

1. Calculate your income: The first step in creating a budget is to calculate your total income. This includes any money you earn from your job or other sources, such as rental income or investment dividends.

2. Track your expenses: The next step is to track your expenses over a period of time, such as a month. This will give you a sense of how much you are spending in various categories, such as housing, transportation, food, entertainment, and so on.

3. Categorize your expenses: Once you have tracked your expenses, categorize them into different categories, such as housing, transportation, food, entertainment, and so on. This will help you see where your money is going and identify areas where you may be able to cut back on expenses.

4. Determine your fixed and variable expenses: Fixed expenses are those that remain the same from month to month, such as rent or mortgage payments, car payments, and insurance premiums. Variable expenses are

those that can fluctuate from month to month, such as groceries, utilities, and entertainment. Understanding your fixed and variable expenses will help you create a more accurate budget.

5. Set financial goals: Determine your short-term and long-term financial goals, such as saving for a down payment on a house, paying off credit card debt, or saving for retirement. Your budget should be designed to help you achieve these goals.

6. Allocate your income: Once you have a clear sense of your income, expenses, and financial goals, allocate your income to different categories. Start with your fixed expenses, such as rent or mortgage payments, car payments, and insurance premiums. Then allocate money towards your variable expenses, such as groceries, utilities, and entertainment. Finally, allocate money towards your financial goals, such as saving for a down payment on a house or paying off credit card debt.

7. Monitor your budget: Once you have created your budget, it's important to monitor your spending and savings over time. Review your budget on a regular basis to ensure that you are staying on track with your financial goals, and make adjustments as needed.

In addition to these steps, there are several tips to keep in mind when creating a personalized budget:

8. Be realistic: Your budget should be based on your actual income and expenses, not on what you wish they were. Be honest with yourself about your financial situation, and create a budget that reflects your actual income and expenses.

9. Be flexible: Your budget should be flexible enough to accommodate unexpected expenses or changes in your income. Build in a cushion for

unexpected expenses, and be prepared to make adjustments to your budget as needed.

10. Be disciplined: Stick to your budget as closely as possible, and avoid overspending in any category. Use cash instead of credit cards to help you stay on track with your spending.

11. Prioritize your financial goals: Your budget should be designed to help you achieve your financial goals. Make sure that you are allocating enough money towards your goals, and be willing to make sacrifices in other areas in order to achieve your goals.

In conclusion, creating a personalized budget is a critical step towards achieving financial stability and saving money. By calculating your income, tracking your expenses, categorizing your expenses, determining your fixed and variable expenses, setting financial goals, allocating your income, and monitoring your budget, you can create a budget that reflects your individual circumstances and financial goals.

Evaluating Your Income and Expenses

Evaluating your income and expenses is an important step towards achieving financial stability and saving money. Understanding your cash flow is crucial in identifying where you can cut back and how much you can realistically save each month. In this essay, we will discuss how to evaluate your income and expenses to create a solid foundation for your financial goals.

Income Evaluation

The first step in evaluating your income is to determine your gross income, which is the amount you earn before taxes and other deductions. Your gross income can come from your job or from other sources such as rental income or investment dividends.

Next, you need to determine your net income, which is the amount you actually receive after taxes and other deductions. Your net income is the amount you have available to pay for your expenses and save each month.

To evaluate your income, you should also consider the stability of your income sources. If you have a job with a stable salary, your income is likely to be predictable each month. However, if you are self-employed or work in a field with irregular income, you may need to take extra precautions to ensure that you have enough money to cover your expenses each month.

Expense Evaluation

The next step is to evaluate your expenses. To do this, you will need to track your expenses over a period of time, such as a month. This will help you see where your money is going and identify areas where you can cut back on expenses.

Start by categorizing your expenses into different categories, such as housing, transportation, food, entertainment, and so on. This will help you see where your money is going and identify areas where you can cut back on expenses.

Next, determine your fixed and variable expenses. Fixed expenses are those that remain the same from month to month, such as rent or mortgage payments, car payments, and insurance premiums. Variable expenses are those that can fluctuate from month to month, such as groceries, utilities, and entertainment.

Once you have a clear sense of your income and expenses, you can start to evaluate your budget. This will help you see where you can cut back on expenses and how much you can realistically save each month.

Identifying Areas to Cut Back

To evaluate your budget and identify areas where you can cut back on expenses, start by looking at your variable expenses. Are there any areas where you are spending more than you need to? For example, are you eating out too often, or spending too much on entertainment or shopping? If so, look for ways to cut back in these areas.

Next, look at your fixed expenses. Are there any opportunities to reduce your expenses, such as refinancing your mortgage or car loan? Can you negotiate lower rates with your insurance providers? Look for ways to save money on your fixed expenses without sacrificing quality.

Finally, look for ways to increase your income. Can you take on a side job or start a business? Can you negotiate a raise at work or take on extra hours? Increasing your income can help you achieve your financial goals faster and make it easier to save money each month.

In conclusion, evaluating your income and expenses is an important step towards achieving financial stability and saving money. By understanding your cash flow, categorizing your expenses, and identifying areas to cut back on expenses, you can create a budget that reflects your financial goals and helps you achieve them. By being proactive in managing your finances and making adjustments as needed, you can build a solid foundation for your financial future.

Setting Realistic Savings Goals

Setting realistic savings goals is an essential step in achieving financial stability and security. However, setting goals that are too ambitious can be discouraging and lead to frustration and burnout. In this essay, we will discuss how to set realistic savings goals that are achievable and motivating.

Determine your financial priorities

The first step in setting realistic savings goals is to determine your financial priorities. Ask yourself what is most important to you financially. Do you want to pay off debt? Save for a down payment on a house? Build an emergency fund? Save for retirement? Determine your priorities, and then focus on setting goals that will help you achieve them.

Assess your current financial situation

Once you have determined your financial priorities, assess your current financial situation. How much money do you have in savings? How much do you owe in debt? What are your monthly expenses? Assessing your current financial situation will help you set realistic savings goals that are achievable based on your income and expenses.

Set specific and measurable goals

When setting savings goals, be specific and measurable. Instead of setting a goal to "save more money," set a specific goal, such as "save $500 per month." This will make it easier to track your progress and stay motivated. Make sure your goals are also realistic based on your current financial situation and income.

Break down long-term goals into smaller milestones

If your long-term goal is to save for a down payment on a house or retirement, break it down into smaller milestones. For example, set a goal to save 10% of your income each month, or to save a specific amount each year. Breaking down long-term goals into smaller milestones makes them more manageable and helps you stay motivated.

Consider the time frame

When setting savings goals, consider the time frame. Short-term goals, such as building an emergency fund, may have a shorter time frame, while long-term goals, such as saving for retirement, may take years or even decades. Consider the time frame for your goals and adjust them accordingly.

Be flexible

Be flexible when setting savings goals. Life can be unpredictable, and unexpected expenses or changes in your income can affect your ability to save. If you encounter unexpected challenges, be flexible and adjust your goals as needed. Don't give up on your goals, but be willing to make adjustments as necessary.

Celebrate your successes

Finally, celebrate your successes along the way. When you reach a savings milestone or achieve a financial goal, take time to acknowledge and celebrate your success. Celebrating your successes can help you stay motivated and focused on achieving your next goal.

In conclusion, setting realistic savings goals is an essential step in achieving financial stability and security. By determining your financial priorities, assessing your current financial situation, setting specific and measurable goals, breaking down long-term goals into smaller milestones, considering the time frame, being flexible, and celebrating your successes, you can set realistic savings goals that are achievable and motivating. With patience, discipline, and a clear plan, you can achieve your financial goals and build a brighter financial future.

Tracking Your Spending and Adjusting Your Budget

Tracking your spending and adjusting your budget are essential steps towards achieving financial stability and saving money. By tracking your spending, you can identify areas where you can cut back on expenses and make adjustments to your budget. In this essay, we will discuss how to track your spending and adjust your budget to achieve your financial goals.

Use a budgeting app or spreadsheet

The first step in tracking your spending is to use a budgeting app or spreadsheet to record your income and expenses. This will help you see where your money is going and identify areas where you can cut back on expenses. There are many free budgeting apps available that can help you track your spending and stay on top of your finances.

Categorize your expenses

Categorize your expenses into different categories, such as housing, transportation, food, entertainment, and so on. This will help you see where your money is going and identify areas where you can cut back on expenses. You can also use subcategories to further break down your expenses and identify specific areas where you can save money.

Monitor your spending

Monitor your spending on a regular basis, such as weekly or monthly, to ensure that you are staying on track with your budget. This will help you identify areas where you may be overspending and make adjustments to your budget as needed.

Identify areas to cut back

Identify areas where you can cut back on expenses, such as eating out less, shopping for sales, or reducing your utility bills. Use your budgeting app or spreadsheet to identify specific areas where you can save money and adjust your budget accordingly.

Be realistic

Be realistic when setting your budget and goals. Don't set a budget that is too restrictive or unrealistic. Make sure that your budget reflects your actual income and expenses, and allows for unexpected expenses or changes in your income.

Adjust your budget as needed

Adjust your budget as needed based on changes in your income or expenses. If you receive a raise at work, consider increasing your savings or reducing your debt. If you have unexpected expenses, adjust your budget to accommodate them.

Prioritize your financial goals

Make sure that your budget reflects your financial goals. Prioritize your financial goals and make sure that you are allocating enough money towards them. Be willing to make sacrifices in other areas in order to achieve your goals.

In conclusion, tracking your spending and adjusting your budget are essential steps towards achieving financial stability and saving money. By using a budgeting app or spreadsheet, categorizing your expenses, monitoring your spending, identifying areas to cut back, being realistic, adjusting your budget as needed, and prioritizing your financial goals, you can create a budget that reflects your individual circumstances and financial goals. With patience, discipline, and a clear plan, you can achieve your financial goals and build a brighter financial future.

Chapter Three

Reducing Expenses

Reducing expenses is an important step towards achieving financial stability and saving money. By identifying areas where you can cut back on expenses, you can free up money for savings or other financial goals. In this essay, we will discuss several ways to reduce expenses and save money.

Create a budget

Creating a budget is a critical step in reducing expenses. By tracking your income and expenses, you can identify areas where you are overspending and make adjustments to your budget accordingly. Start by categorizing your expenses into different categories, such as housing, transportation, food, entertainment, and so on. Then allocate your income towards these categories, with a focus on reducing expenses in areas where you are overspending.

Cut back on discretionary expenses

Discretionary expenses are expenses that are not necessary for your basic needs, such as entertainment, shopping, or eating out. Cutting back on discretionary expenses can help you save a significant amount of money each month. Start by identifying areas where you can reduce your discretionary spending, such as by eating out less or shopping for sales.

Reduce your utility bills

Reducing your utility bills can also help you save money. Start by making small changes, such as turning off lights when you leave a room, using energy-efficient light bulbs, and turning off electronics when they are not in use. You can also consider making larger changes, such as installing a programmable thermostat or investing in energy-efficient appliances.

Negotiate your bills

Negotiating your bills can also help you save money. Call your service providers, such as your cable or internet provider, and ask if they can reduce your bill. You may be surprised at how willing they are to work with you to keep your business.

Shop for sales and discounts

Shopping for sales and discounts can also help you save money. Before making a purchase, research prices online and look for coupons or discounts. You can also consider buying used items or shopping at thrift stores to save money on clothing or household items.

Buy in bulk

Buying in bulk can also help you save money on groceries and household items. Look for sales on non-perishable items, such as canned goods or toilet paper, and buy in bulk to save money over time.

Use cash instead of credit cards

Using cash instead of credit cards can also help you reduce expenses. When you pay with cash, you are more likely to be mindful of your spending and less likely to overspend. You can also use cash envelopes to allocate money towards different categories, such as groceries or entertainment, and avoid overspending in any one category.

In conclusion, reducing expenses is an important step towards achieving financial stability and saving money. By creating a budget, cutting back on discretionary expenses, reducing your utility bills, negotiating your bills, shopping for sales and discounts, buying in bulk, and using cash instead of credit cards, you can free up money for savings or other financial goals. With patience, discipline, and a clear plan, you can achieve your financial goals and build a brighter financial future.

Cutting Back on Housing Costs

Cutting back on housing costs is one of the most effective ways to save money and achieve financial stability. Housing expenses can be a significant portion of your monthly budget, so reducing them can make a big difference in your finances. In this essay, we will discuss several ways to cut back on housing costs and save money.

Downsize your living space

One of the most effective ways to cut back on housing costs is to downsize your living space. Moving to a smaller home or apartment can significantly reduce your housing expenses. Consider downsizing if you are living in a home that is larger than you need, or if you are paying for amenities or features that you don't use or need.

Look for a cheaper location

Another way to cut back on housing costs is to look for a cheaper location. Consider moving to a less expensive neighborhood or city, or to a location that is closer to your job or other daily activities. Moving to a cheaper location can help you save money on rent or mortgage payments, as well as on transportation costs.

Find a roommate

Finding a roommate is another way to cut back on housing costs. Sharing rent or mortgage payments with someone else can significantly reduce your housing expenses. Look for a roommate who shares your values and lifestyle, and who is reliable and responsible.

Negotiate your rent or mortgage

Negotiating your rent or mortgage can also help you save money on housing costs. If you are renting, ask your landlord if they are willing to lower your rent, or if they can offer any incentives or discounts. If you are a homeowner, consider refinancing your mortgage or negotiating with your lender to lower your interest rate or monthly payment.

Consider alternative housing options

Consider alternative housing options, such as living in a tiny home, a trailer, or a converted garage or shed. These alternative housing options can be significantly less expensive than traditional homes or apartments, and can be a great way to save money on housing costs.

Reduce your utility bills

Reducing your utility bills can also help you save money on housing costs. Start by making small changes, such as turning off lights when you leave a room, using energy-efficient light bulbs, and turning off electronics when they are not in use. You can also consider making larger changes, such as installing a programmable thermostat or investing in energy-efficient appliances.

Do your own repairs and maintenance

Doing your own repairs and maintenance can also help you save money on housing costs. Learn how to fix basic household problems, such as plumbing or electrical issues, and invest in the tools and supplies you need to do the repairs yourself. This can save you money on repair bills and can also help you become more self-sufficient.

In conclusion, cutting back on housing costs is an effective way to save money and achieve financial stability. By downsizing your living space, looking for a cheaper location, finding a roommate, negotiating your rent or mortgage, considering alternative housing options, reducing your utility bills, and doing your own repairs and maintenance, you can significantly reduce your housing expenses and free up money for other financial goals. With patience, discipline, and a clear plan, you can achieve your financial goals and build a brighter financial future.

Saving Money on Food and Groceries

Saving money on food and groceries is a great way to reduce your expenses and save money. Groceries can be a significant part of your monthly budget, but there are many ways to cut back on food costs without sacrificing quality or nutrition. In this essay, we will discuss several ways to save money on food and groceries.

Plan your meals and shop with a list

One of the best ways to save money on food and groceries is to plan your meals in advance and shop with a list. Before you go grocery shopping, make a list of the items you need and stick to it. This will help you avoid impulse purchases and ensure that you buy only the items you need.

Shop for sales and use coupons

Shopping for sales and using coupons is another effective way to save money on food and groceries. Look for sales and discounts on items you need, and use coupons to save even more money. You can also consider buying generic or store-brand items, which are often less expensive than name-brand items.

Buy in bulk

Buying in bulk can also help you save money on food and groceries. Look for sales on non-perishable items, such as canned goods or toilet paper, and buy in bulk to save money over time. You can also consider buying in bulk from discount stores or online retailers.

Cook at home

Cooking at home is a great way to save money on food and groceries. Eating out or ordering takeout can be expensive, so consider cooking meals at home instead. You can also meal prep in advance to save time and ensure that you have healthy, affordable meals throughout the week.

Use leftovers

Using leftovers is another way to save money on food and groceries. Instead of throwing away leftovers, use them to make new meals or snacks. You can also freeze leftovers for later use, which can help you save money and reduce food waste.

Grow your own food

Growing your own food is another way to save money on food and groceries. Consider starting a garden or growing herbs or vegetables in pots. This can be a fun and rewarding way to save money and enjoy fresh, healthy food.

Reduce food waste

Reducing food waste is also an effective way to save money on food and groceries. Plan your meals in advance to avoid buying more food than you need, and store your food properly to ensure that it lasts longer. You can also repurpose food scraps, such as vegetable peelings, to make homemade broth or compost.

In conclusion, saving money on food and groceries is a great way to reduce your expenses and achieve financial stability. By planning your meals and shopping with a list, shopping for sales and using coupons, buying in bulk, cooking at home, using leftovers, growing your own food, and reducing food waste, you can significantly reduce your food expenses and free up money for other financial goals. With patience, discipline, and a clear plan, you can achieve your financial goals and build a brighter financial future.

Reducing Transportation and Travel Expenses

Reducing transportation and travel expenses is an effective way to save money and achieve financial stability. Transportation and travel expenses can be a significant portion of your monthly budget, so reducing them can make a big difference in your finances. In this essay, we will discuss several ways to reduce transportation and travel expenses and save money.

Use public transportation

Using public transportation is one of the best ways to reduce transportation expenses. Public transportation, such as buses, trains, or subways, is often less expensive than driving a car or taking a taxi. Consider using public transportation for your daily commute or for running errands, and look for discounts or special offers that can help you save even more money.

Walk or bike

Walking or biking is another way to reduce transportation expenses. If you live close to your workplace or other daily activities, consider walking or biking instead of driving or using public transportation. This can save you money on gas, parking, or transit fares, and can also help you stay healthy and active.

Carpool or rideshare

Carpooling or ridesharing is another effective way to reduce transportation expenses. Find friends or colleagues who live or work near you and carpool to work or other daily activities. You can also use ridesharing services, such as Uber or Lyft, to save money on transportation costs.

Maintain your vehicle

Maintaining your vehicle is also important for reducing transportation expenses. Regular maintenance, such as oil changes or tire rotations, can help you avoid costly repairs or breakdowns. Keeping your tires inflated and driving at a moderate speed can also help you save money on gas.

Avoid unnecessary travel

Avoiding unnecessary travel is another way to reduce travel expenses. If you are planning a trip, consider whether it is really necessary or if you can postpone it. You can also consider virtual meetings or conferences instead of traveling to them in person.

Use travel rewards and discounts

Using travel rewards and discounts can also help you save money on travel expenses. Look for credit cards or loyalty programs that offer travel rewards, such as airline miles or hotel points, and use them to save money on future travel. You can also look for discounts on travel websites or through travel agencies.

Travel during off-peak times

Traveling during off-peak times can also help you save money on travel expenses. Flights and hotels are often less expensive during off-peak times, such as during weekdays or during non-holiday periods. Consider traveling during these times to save money on travel expenses.

In conclusion, reducing transportation and travel expenses is an effective way to save money and achieve financial stability. By using public transportation, walking or biking, carpooling or ridesharing, maintaining your vehicle, avoiding unnecessary travel, using travel rewards and discounts, and traveling during off-peak times, you can significantly reduce your transportation and travel expenses and free up money for other financial goals. With patience, discipline, and a clear plan, you can achieve your financial goals and build a brighter financial future.

Chapter Four

Smart Shopping Habits

Smart shopping habits are essential for saving money and achieving financial stability. Whether you are buying groceries, clothes, or household items, there are many ways to shop smart and save money. In this essay, we will discuss several smart shopping habits that can help you save money and achieve your financial goals.

Make a list and stick to it

One of the best smart shopping habits is to make a list and stick to it. Before you go shopping, make a list of the items you need and stick to it. This will help you avoid impulse purchases and ensure that you buy only the items you need. It can also help you save time and reduce stress during shopping trips.

Look for sales and discounts

Looking for sales and discounts is another effective smart shopping habit. Look for sales and discounts on the items you need, and consider buying in bulk or waiting for a sale to make a purchase. You can also use coupons or discount codes to save money on your purchases.

Compare prices

Comparing prices is also an important smart shopping habit. Look for the best prices on the items you need, and consider buying from different stores or online retailers to save money. You can also use price comparison websites or apps to find the best deals.

Buy generic or store-brand items

Buying generic or store-brand items is another smart shopping habit that can help you save money. These items are often less expensive than name-brand items, but can be just as good in terms of quality and effectiveness. Consider buying generic or store-brand items for non-perishable items, such as cleaning products or canned goods.

Avoid shopping when hungry

Avoiding shopping when hungry is a smart shopping habit that can help you save money. When you are hungry, you may be more likely to make impulse purchases or buy unnecessary items. Eat a snack or meal before you go shopping to reduce the likelihood of making these types of purchases.

Avoid buying items you don't need

Avoiding buying items you don't need is another smart shopping habit that can help you save money. Before you make a purchase, ask yourself whether you really need the item or whether you can do without it. This can help you avoid unnecessary purchases and save money over time.

Shop out of season

Shopping out of season is a smart shopping habit that can help you save money on seasonal items, such as clothing or decorations. Consider buying these items during the off-season when they are less expensive, and store them until you need them.

In conclusion, smart shopping habits are essential for saving money and achieving financial stability. By making a list and sticking to it, looking for sales and discounts, comparing prices, buying generic or store-brand items, avoiding shopping when hungry, avoiding buying items you don't need, and shopping out of season, you can significantly reduce your expenses and free up money for other financial goals. With patience, discipline, and a clear plan, you can achieve your financial goals and build a brighter financial future.

Finding the Best Deals and Discounts

Finding the best deals and discounts is a crucial aspect of saving money and achieving financial stability. There are numerous ways to find great deals and discounts on various products and services, from groceries and clothing to electronics and travel. In this essay, we will discuss several effective strategies for finding the best deals and discounts and saving money.

Use comparison websites and apps

Comparison websites and apps can be incredibly helpful in finding the best deals and discounts. These platforms allow you to compare prices across different retailers or service providers, and find the best deals available. Some popular comparison websites and apps include PriceGrabber, Shopzilla, and Google Shopping.

Sign up for newsletters and emails

Many retailers and service providers offer exclusive deals and discounts to subscribers of their newsletters and email lists. Sign up for these newsletters and emails to stay informed about the latest promotions and discounts. You can also consider creating a separate email address for these types of communications to avoid cluttering your primary inbox.

Use cashback apps and websites

Cashback apps and websites offer rewards or cashback for shopping at certain retailers or using specific services. These rewards can add up over time and help you save money on your purchases. Some popular cashback apps and websites include Rakuten, Swagbucks, and Honey.

Check for discounts and coupons online

Before making a purchase, always check online for available discounts and coupons. Retailers and service providers often offer coupons or promo codes that can save you money on your purchase. Websites like Coup ons.com and RetailMeNot are great resources for finding these types of discounts.

Look for clearance sales and seasonal discounts

Clearance sales and seasonal discounts can be great opportunities to save money on products or services. Look for clearance sales at retailers and check for seasonal discounts, such as end-of-season sales, back-to-school sales, and holiday sales.

Consider buying used or refurbished items

Buying used or refurbished items can be an effective way to save money. Websites like eBay and Craigslist are great resources for finding used or refurbished items at discounted prices. Just be sure to research the seller and the condition of the item before making a purchase.

Use credit card rewards and loyalty programs

Credit card rewards and loyalty programs can also help you save money on your purchases. Look for credit cards or loyalty programs that offer rewards or cashback on your purchases, and use them to save money over time. Just be sure to pay off your credit card balance in full each month to avoid interest charges.

In conclusion, finding the best deals and discounts is an essential strategy for saving money and achieving financial stability. By using comparison websites and apps, signing up for newsletters and emails, using cashback apps and websites, checking for discounts and coupons online, looking for clearance sales and seasonal discounts, considering buying used or refurbished items, and using credit card rewards and loyalty programs, you can significantly reduce your expenses and free up money for other financial goals. With patience, discipline, and a clear plan, you can achieve your financial goals and build a brighter financial future.

Utilizing Coupons and Cashback Programs

Utilizing coupons and cashback programs can be an effective way to save money on your purchases and achieve financial stability. Coupons and cashback programs can help you reduce your expenses and free up money for other financial goals. In this essay, we will discuss several effective strategies for utilizing coupons and cashback programs and saving money.

Look for coupons in-store and online

One of the easiest ways to utilize coupons is to look for them in-store or online. Many retailers offer coupons that can be used in-store or online, and these can help you save money on your purchases. Check the retailer's website or social media pages for available coupons or visit coupon websites like Coupons.com or RetailMeNot to find discounts for various retailers.

Sign up for loyalty programs

Many retailers offer loyalty programs that provide rewards or discounts to members. Sign up for these loyalty programs to receive exclusive discounts and offers. Some popular loyalty programs include Amazon Prime, Target Circle, and CVS ExtraCare.

Use cashback apps and websites

Cashback apps and websites offer rewards or cashback for shopping at certain retailers or using specific services. These rewards can add up over time and help you save money on your purchases. Some popular cashback apps and websites include Rakuten, Swagbucks, and Honey.

Use credit card rewards

Credit card rewards can also help you save money on your purchases. Look for credit cards that offer rewards or cashback on your purchases, and use them to save money over time. Just be sure to pay off your credit card balance in full each month to avoid interest charges.

Look for deals on bulk purchases

Buying in bulk can also help you save money on your purchases. Look for deals on bulk purchases at retailers like Costco, Sam's Club, or BJ's Wholesale Club. Buying in bulk can be particularly useful for non-perishable items, such as toilet paper, cleaning supplies, or canned goods.

Plan your purchases around sale events

Many retailers offer sale events throughout the year, such as Black Friday or Cyber Monday. Plan your purchases around these sale events to take advantage of discounts and offers. You can also look for seasonal sales or clearance events to save money on your purchases.

Use coupons for dining and entertainment

Coupons can also be useful for dining and entertainment. Look for coupons for restaurants, movie theaters, or amusement parks to save money on these activities. You can also use apps like Groupon or LivingSocial to find discounts for various activities and events.

In conclusion, utilizing coupons and cashback programs can be an effective way to save money on your purchases and achieve financial stability. By looking for coupons in-store and online, signing up for loyalty programs, using cashback apps and websites, using credit card rewards, looking for deals on bulk purchases, planning your purchases around sale events, and using coupons for dining and entertainment, you can significantly reduce your expenses and free up money for other financial goals. With patience, discipline, and a clear plan, you can achieve your financial goals and build a brighter financial future.

Shopping Secondhand and Thrift Stores

Shopping secondhand and thrift stores is a great way to save money and achieve financial stability. Secondhand and thrift stores offer a wide range of items, from clothing and accessories to furniture and home decor, at discounted prices. In this essay, we will discuss several effective strategies for shopping secondhand and thrift stores and saving money.

Look for quality items

When shopping at secondhand and thrift stores, it's important to look for quality items. Inspect the items carefully for signs of wear or damage, and make sure they are in good condition. Focus on buying items that are well-made and durable, even if they cost a little more than other items in the store.

Shop frequently

Shopping frequently is another effective strategy for finding great deals at secondhand and thrift stores. These stores receive new items regularly, so it's important to check back often to find new items and take advantage of discounts and sales.

Know what you're looking for

Having a clear idea of what you're looking for can help you save time and money when shopping at secondhand and thrift stores. Make a list of the items you need or want, and focus on finding those items during your shopping trips. This can help you avoid impulse purchases and ensure that you buy only the items you need.

Shop at different stores

Shopping at different secondhand and thrift stores can also help you find great deals and unique items. Each store has its own inventory and pricing, so it's worth checking out different stores in your area to find the best deals and selection.

Take advantage of sales and discounts

Many secondhand and thrift stores offer sales and discounts on their items. Look for signs or ask the store employees about any current promotions or discounts. Some stores may also offer special discounts for students, seniors, or military members.

Consider alterations and DIY projects

If you find an item that you love but it doesn't fit perfectly or needs some repairs, consider doing alterations or DIY projects to make it work. Alterations or repairs can be less expensive than buying a new item, and can help you create a unique and personalized piece.

Donate or sell your own items

Donating or selling your own items to secondhand and thrift stores can also be a great way to save money and reduce clutter in your home. Many stores offer trade-in or consignment programs where you can sell your own items in exchange for store credit or cash.

In conclusion, shopping secondhand and thrift stores is an effective way to save money and achieve financial stability. By looking for quality items, shopping frequently, knowing what you're looking for, shopping at different stores, taking advantage of sales and discounts, considering alterations and DIY projects, and donating or selling your own items, you can significantly reduce your expenses and free up money for other financial goals. With patience, discipline, and a clear plan, you can achieve your financial goals and build a brighter financial future.

Chapter Five

Managing Debt and Credit

Managing debt and credit is an essential aspect of achieving financial stability and saving money. Debt and credit can have a significant impact on your financial situation, and it's important to understand how to manage them effectively. In this essay, we will discuss several effective strategies for managing debt and credit and saving money.

Know your credit score

Your credit score is a crucial factor in managing debt and credit. Your credit score can affect your ability to get loans, credit cards, and mortgages, and can also affect the interest rates and terms of these financial products. Know your credit score and monitor it regularly to ensure that it is accurate and up-to-date.

Pay your bills on time

Paying your bills on time is another essential strategy for managing debt and credit. Late payments can damage your credit score and result in additional fees and penalties. Set up automatic payments or reminders to ensure that you pay your bills on time each month.

Create a budget

Creating a budget is an effective way to manage your debt and credit. A budget can help you track your income and expenses, and ensure that you have enough money to pay your bills and debts each month. Be sure to include all of your debts and credit card balances in your budget to ensure that you are paying them off effectively.

Prioritize debt repayment

Prioritizing debt repayment is another effective strategy for managing debt and credit. Focus on paying off high-interest debt first, such as credit card balances, to reduce the amount of interest you pay over time. Once you have paid off high-interest debt, you can focus on other debts, such as student loans or mortgages.

Negotiate lower interest rates

Negotiating lower interest rates on your debts and credit cards can also help you save money. Contact your lenders or credit card companies and ask if they can lower your interest rate. If you have a good credit score and a history of on-time payments, you may be able to negotiate a lower rate.

Consider debt consolidation

Debt consolidation can be a useful strategy for managing multiple debts. With debt consolidation, you combine multiple debts into one loan with a lower interest rate. This can make it easier to manage your debts and save money on interest over time.

Use credit cards responsibly

Using credit cards responsibly is another essential strategy for managing debt and credit. Use your credit cards only for necessary purchases, and pay off the balances in full each month to avoid interest charges. Avoid maxing out your credit cards or using them for cash advances, which can result in additional fees and damage your credit score.

In conclusion, managing debt and credit is an essential aspect of achieving financial stability and saving money. By knowing your credit score, paying your bills on time, creating a budget, prioritizing debt repayment, negotiating lower interest rates, considering debt consolidation, and using credit cards responsibly, you can effectively manage your debt and credit and build a brighter financial future. With patience, discipline, and a clear plan, you can achieve your financial goals and become financially stable.

Strategies for Paying Off High-Interest Debt

High-interest debt can be a significant financial burden, affecting your credit score and costing you hundreds or even thousands of dollars in interest charges. However, there are several effective strategies for paying off high-interest debt and achieving financial stability. In this essay, we will discuss several effective strategies for paying off high-interest debt and saving money.

Make a budget

Creating a budget is an essential first step in paying off high-interest debt. A budget can help you track your income and expenses, and ensure that you have enough money to pay your bills and debts each month. Be sure to include all of your debts and credit card balances in your budget to ensure that you are paying them off effectively.

Prioritize your debts

Prioritizing your debts is another essential strategy for paying off high-interest debt. Focus on paying off high-interest debt first, such as credit card balances, to reduce the amount of interest you pay over time. Once you have paid off high-interest debt, you can focus on other debts, such as student loans or mortgages.

Consider a balance transfer

A balance transfer can be a useful strategy for paying off high-interest debt. With a balance transfer, you transfer your high-interest credit card balance to a credit card with a lower interest rate. This can help you save money on interest charges and pay off your debt more quickly. Be sure to read the terms and conditions of the balance transfer carefully, and be aware of any fees or restrictions.

Increase your income

Increasing your income is another effective strategy for paying off high-interest debt. Look for ways to increase your income, such as taking on a side job or selling unwanted items. Use the extra income to pay off your high-interest debt more quickly.

Cut your expenses

Cutting your expenses can also help you pay off high-interest debt more quickly. Look for ways to reduce your monthly expenses, such as cutting back on dining out or entertainment. Use the money you save to pay off your high-interest debt.

Use the snowball method

The snowball method is a debt repayment strategy that involves paying off your smallest debts first, then moving on to larger debts. With the snowball method, you make minimum payments on all of your debts except the smallest one, which you pay off as quickly as possible. Once you have paid off the smallest debt, you move on to the next smallest debt and continue the process. This can help you build momentum and stay motivated as you pay off your debts.

Seek help from a financial advisor

If you are struggling to pay off high-interest debt, consider seeking help from a financial advisor. A financial advisor can help you create a debt repayment plan that fits your individual needs and circumstances. They can also provide advice on budgeting, saving, and investing to help you achieve your financial goals.

In conclusion, paying off high-interest debt is an essential aspect of achieving financial stability and saving money. By making a budget, prioritizing your debts, considering a balance transfer, increasing your income, cutting your expenses, using the snowball method, and seeking help from a financial advisor, you can effectively pay off your high-interest debt and build a brighter financial future. With patience, discipline, and a clear plan, you can achieve your financial goals and become financially stable.

Building and Maintaining Good Credit

Building and maintaining good credit is essential for achieving financial stability and saving money. Your credit score can affect your ability to get loans, credit cards, and mortgages, and can also affect the interest rates and terms of these financial products. In this essay, we will discuss several effective strategies for building and maintaining good credit and saving money.

Pay your bills on time

Paying your bills on time is the most important factor in building and maintaining good credit. Late payments can damage your credit score and make it more difficult to get loans and credit in the future. Set up automatic payments or reminders to ensure that you pay your bills on time each month.

Keep your credit card balances low

Keeping your credit card balances low is another essential strategy for building and maintaining good credit. High credit card balances can increase your debt-to-credit ratio and lower your credit score. Aim to keep your credit card balances below 30% of your credit limit.

Monitor your credit report

Monitoring your credit report regularly can help you detect errors or inaccuracies that could be hurting your credit score. You can get a free credit report from each of the three major credit bureaus (Equifax, Experian, and TransUnion) once a year. Review your credit report carefully and report any errors or inaccuracies to the credit bureau.

Use credit cards responsibly

Using credit cards responsibly is another important factor in building and maintaining good credit. Use your credit cards only for necessary purchases, and pay off the balances in full each month to avoid interest charges. Avoid maxing out your credit cards or using them for cash advances, which can result in additional fees and damage your credit score.

Keep old credit accounts open

Keeping old credit accounts open can help you build and maintain good credit. Length of credit history is a factor in determining your credit score, so keeping old accounts open can help you establish a long credit history. Be sure to use the accounts occasionally to keep them active.

Apply for credit sparingly

Applying for credit too often can hurt your credit score. Each time you apply for credit, it can result in a hard inquiry on your credit report, which can lower your score. Only apply for credit when you need it, and be selective about the credit products you apply for.

Consider a secured credit card

If you are struggling to get approved for a traditional credit card, a secured credit card can be a useful option. A secured credit card requires a security deposit, which serves as collateral for the credit card issuer. Using a secured credit card responsibly can help you build or rebuild your credit.

In conclusion, building and maintaining good credit is essential for achieving financial stability and saving money. By paying your bills on time, keeping your credit card balances low, monitoring your credit report, using credit cards responsibly, keeping old credit accounts open, applying for credit sparingly, and considering a secured credit card, you can effectively build and maintain good credit and achieve your financial goals. With patience, discipline, and a clear plan, you can build a brighter financial future.

Avoiding Common Credit Pitfalls

Credit can be a valuable financial tool, allowing you to make large purchases and build a positive credit history. However, there are several common credit pitfalls that can damage your credit score, cost you money, and lead to financial instability. In this essay, we will discuss several common credit pitfalls and strategies for avoiding them to save money and achieve financial stability.

Maxing out credit cards

Maxing out credit cards is one of the most common credit pitfalls. High credit card balances can increase your debt-to-credit ratio and lower your credit score. Additionally, carrying a high balance can result in significant interest charges over time. To avoid this pitfall, aim to keep your credit card balances below 30% of your credit limit.

Missing payments

Missing payments is another common credit pitfall that can damage your credit score and result in additional fees and penalties. Set up automatic payments or reminders to ensure that you pay your bills on time each month. If you do miss a payment, contact your creditor or lender as soon as possible to try to resolve the issue.

Applying for too much credit

Applying for too much credit can also hurt your credit score. Each time you apply for credit, it can result in a hard inquiry on your credit report, which can lower your score. Only apply for credit when you need it, and be selective about the credit products you apply for.

Closing old credit accounts

Closing old credit accounts can also hurt your credit score. Length of credit history is a factor in determining your credit score, so closing old accounts can reduce the length of your credit history. Additionally, closing an account can increase your debt-to-credit ratio if you have balances on other accounts. Keep old accounts open and use them occasionally to keep them active.

Not monitoring your credit report

Not monitoring your credit report regularly can result in errors or inaccuracies that could be hurting your credit score. You can get a free credit report from each of the three major credit bureaus (Equifax, Experian, and TransUnion) once a year. Review your credit report carefully and report any errors or inaccuracies to the credit bureau.

Falling for credit repair scams

Credit repair scams are another common credit pitfall. These scams promise to remove negative items from your credit report or improve your credit score quickly and easily. However, many of these scams are fraudulent and can result in additional fees and damage to your credit score. Be wary of any company that promises to improve your credit score quickly and do your research before hiring a credit repair company.

Not understanding your credit card terms

Not understanding your credit card terms can result in additional fees and penalties. Be sure to read your credit card agreement carefully and understand the interest rates, fees, and penalties associated with your card. Avoid using your credit card for cash advances or balance transfers, which can result in additional fees and higher interest rates.

In conclusion, avoiding common credit pitfalls is essential for achieving financial stability and saving money. By avoiding maxing out credit cards, missing payments, applying for too much credit, closing old credit accounts, not monitoring your credit report, falling for credit repair scams, and understanding your credit card terms, you can effectively manage your credit and build a brighter financial future. With patience, discipline, and a clear plan, you can achieve your financial goals and become financially stable.

Chapter Six

Saving on Utilities and Household Expenses

Saving on utilities and household expenses is an effective way to save money and increase your financial stability. By reducing your energy and water usage, and finding ways to cut back on household expenses, you can free up more money for savings or paying down debt. In this essay, we will discuss several strategies for saving on utilities and household expenses.

Use energy-efficient appliances and light bulbs

Using energy-efficient appliances and light bulbs can help you save on your energy bills. Look for appliances and light bulbs with the ENERGY STAR label, which indicates that they meet energy efficiency guidelines set by the U.S. Environmental Protection Agency. ENERGY STAR appliances use 10-50% less energy than standard appliances, and ENERGY STAR light bulbs use 75% less energy and last 10-25 times longer than traditional bulbs.

Seal air leaks

Air leaks in your home can cause your heating and cooling systems to work harder, leading to higher energy bills. Seal air leaks by caulking or weatherstripping around windows and doors, and add insulation to your attic and walls to keep your home more comfortable and energy-efficient.

Adjust your thermostat

Adjusting your thermostat can also help you save on your energy bills. Set your thermostat to 68 degrees or lower in the winter, and 78 degrees or higher in the summer to reduce your heating and cooling costs. You can also install a programmable thermostat, which will automatically adjust the temperature in your home based on your schedule.

Use water-saving fixtures

Using water-saving fixtures, such as low-flow showerheads and faucets, can help you save on your water bills. These fixtures use less water than traditional fixtures, without sacrificing water pressure or performance. You can also install a low-flow toilet, which uses only 1.6 gallons per flush, compared to the 3.5-7 gallons per flush used by traditional toilets.

Reduce your water usage

Reducing your water usage can also help you save on your water bills. Take shorter showers, turn off the water while brushing your teeth or shaving, and only run your dishwasher and washing machine when you have a full load.

Shop around for insurance

Shopping around for insurance can also help you save on your household expenses. Get quotes from several insurance companies for your home, auto, and other insurance needs, and compare the coverage and costs. You may be able to find a better deal by switching insurance providers.

Cut back on cable and internet

Cutting back on cable and internet can also help you save on your household expenses. Consider reducing your cable package or switching to a streaming service, which can offer a wider variety of programming at a lower cost. You can also shop around for internet providers and switch to a lower-cost plan.

In conclusion, saving on utilities and household expenses is an effective way to save money and increase your financial stability. By using energy-efficient appliances and light bulbs, sealing air leaks, adjusting your thermostat, using water-saving fixtures, reducing your water usage, shopping around for insurance, and cutting back on cable and internet, you can effectively reduce your expenses and free up more money for savings or paying down debt. With patience, discipline, and a clear plan, you can achieve your financial goals and become financially stable.

Energy Efficiency Tips for Your Home

Improving energy efficiency in your home is not only good for the environment, but it can also save you money on your energy bills. By reducing your energy consumption, you can reduce your carbon footprint and contribute to a more sustainable future. In this essay, we will discuss several energy efficiency tips for your home.

Upgrade your insulation

Upgrading your insulation can help you save on your heating and cooling costs. Insulation helps to keep your home warm in the winter and cool in the summer, by trapping heat and preventing it from escaping. Insulation can also reduce noise and improve the overall comfort of your home.

Install energy-efficient windows

Installing energy-efficient windows can also help you save on your heating and cooling costs. Energy-efficient windows are designed to prevent heat transfer, by using multiple panes of glass, low-emissivity coatings, and insulating frames. These windows can reduce your energy consumption and improve the comfort of your home.

Use a programmable thermostat

Using a programmable thermostat can also help you save on your energy bills. A programmable thermostat allows you to set your heating and cooling system to automatically adjust the temperature based on your schedule. This means that you can set your thermostat to reduce energy consumption when you are not at home, or when you are asleep.

Switch to LED light bulbs

Switching to LED light bulbs can also help you save on your energy bills. LED bulbs use significantly less energy than traditional incandescent bulbs, and can last up to 25 times longer. LED bulbs also produce less heat, which can reduce your cooling costs in the summer.

Use energy-efficient appliances

Using energy-efficient appliances can also help you save on your energy bills. Look for appliances with the ENERGY STAR label, which indicates that they meet energy efficiency guidelines set by the U.S. Environmental Protection Agency. ENERGY STAR appliances use 10-50% less energy than standard appliances, and can save you hundreds of dollars on your energy bills over the lifetime of the appliance.

Install a low-flow showerhead

Installing a low-flow showerhead can also help you save on your water and energy bills. Low-flow showerheads use significantly less water than traditional showerheads, without sacrificing water pressure or performance. This means that you can save on your water bills, and reduce the energy needed to heat the water.

Unplug electronics when not in use

Unplugging electronics when they are not in use can also help you save on your energy bills. Many electronics, such as TVs, game consoles, and phone chargers, continue to use energy even when they are not in use. This is known as "phantom" or "standby" power. By unplugging these electronics when they are not in use, you can reduce your energy consumption and save on your energy bills.

In conclusion, improving energy efficiency in your home can help you save money on your energy bills, reduce your carbon footprint, and contribute to a more sustainable future. By upgrading your insulation, installing energy-efficient windows, using a programmable thermostat, switching to LED light bulbs, using energy-efficient appliances, installing a low-flow showerhead, and unplugging electronics when not in use, you can effectively reduce your energy consumption and achieve a more sustainable lifestyle. With patience, discipline, and a clear plan, you can achieve your energy efficiency goals and become a more environmentally conscious consumer.

Reducing Water Usage and Waste

Reducing water usage and waste is not only important for preserving our planet's natural resources, but it can also save you money on your water bill. Water is a finite resource, and as the global population continues to grow, it is becoming increasingly important to use water more efficiently. In this essay, we will discuss several strategies for reducing water usage and waste.

Fix leaks

Fixing leaks is one of the most effective ways to reduce water waste in your home. A single leaky faucet can waste up to 20 gallons of water per day, while a leaky toilet can waste up to 200 gallons per day. Inspect your home regularly for leaks, and fix any leaks as soon as possible to prevent further water waste.

Install low-flow fixtures

Installing low-flow fixtures, such as showerheads and faucets, can help you save on your water bill without sacrificing water pressure or performance. Low-flow fixtures use less water than traditional fixtures, which can add up to significant water savings over time.

Use water-efficient appliances

Using water-efficient appliances, such as washing machines and dishwashers, can also help you save on your water bill. Look for appliances with the ENERGY STAR label, which indicates that they meet energy efficiency guidelines set by the U.S. Environmental Protection Agency. ENERGY STAR appliances use less water than traditional appliances, and can save you money on both your water and energy bills.

Water your lawn efficiently

Watering your lawn efficiently can also help you reduce water usage and waste. Water your lawn early in the morning or late in the evening to prevent water evaporation, and avoid watering on windy days. You can also install a smart irrigation system, which can automatically adjust your watering schedule based on weather conditions and soil moisture.

Use drought-resistant landscaping

Using drought-resistant landscaping, such as native plants and grasses, can also help you reduce water usage and waste. These plants require less water than traditional landscaping, and can still provide a beautiful and sustainable environment for your home.

Collect rainwater

Collecting rainwater can also be an effective way to reduce water usage and waste. You can install a rain barrel to collect rainwater from your roof, which can then be used for watering your lawn or garden. This can help you save on your water bill, while also providing your plants with a natural and sustainable source of water.

Reduce water usage in the kitchen and bathroom

Reducing water usage in the kitchen and bathroom can also help you save on your water bill. You can turn off the water while brushing your teeth or shaving, take shorter showers, and only run your dishwasher and washing machine when you have a full load. These small changes can add up to significant water savings over time.

In conclusion, reducing water usage and waste is not only important for preserving our planet's natural resources, but it can also save you money on your water bill. By fixing leaks, installing low-flow fixtures, using water-efficient appliances, watering your lawn efficiently, using drought-resistant landscaping, collecting rainwater, and reducing water usage in the kitchen and bathroom, you can effectively reduce your water consumption and achieve a more sustainable lifestyle. With patience, discipline, and a clear plan, you can achieve your water conservation goals and become a more environmentally conscious consumer.

Saving Money on Home Maintenance and Repairs

Maintaining and repairing your home can be expensive, but it's an essential part of homeownership. However, there are ways to save money on home maintenance and repairs without sacrificing the quality of the work. In this essay, we will discuss several strategies for saving money on home maintenance and repairs.

Regularly maintain your home

Regularly maintaining your home can help you save money in the long run by preventing major repairs. Schedule regular inspections of your home's major systems, such as your HVAC system, plumbing, and electrical systems. Regularly changing your air filters and cleaning your gutters can also help prevent damage to your home.

Learn basic DIY skills

Learning basic DIY skills can also help you save money on home maintenance and repairs. There are many online resources available, such as YouTube tutorials and online courses, that can teach you how to complete basic home repairs yourself. This can save you money on labor costs and give you a sense of accomplishment.

Shop around for contractors

When you do need to hire a contractor, it's important to shop around and get multiple quotes. This can help you find the best price for the work you need done. Be sure to check reviews and ask for references to ensure you're working with a reputable contractor.

Use quality materials

Using quality materials can also help you save money on home maintenance and repairs in the long run. While cheaper materials may be tempting, they may need to be replaced more frequently, leading to higher overall costs. Using quality materials may cost more upfront, but they will last longer and require fewer repairs over time.

Consider preventative measures

Preventative measures, such as installing gutter guards and trimming trees away from your home, can also help you save money on home maintenance and repairs. These measures can help prevent damage to your home from things like water damage and falling tree limbs.

Maintain a home warranty

Maintaining a home warranty can also help you save money on home maintenance and repairs. Home warranties typically cover major home systems and appliances, and can help offset the cost of repairs or replacement. However, be sure to read the fine print and understand what is and isn't covered by your home warranty.

Take advantage of tax credits

Taking advantage of tax credits for home improvements can also help you save money on home maintenance and repairs. Many home improvements, such as installing energy-efficient windows and HVAC systems, can qualify for tax credits that can help offset the cost of the improvements.

In conclusion, maintaining and repairing your home can be expensive, but there are ways to save money without sacrificing the quality of the work. By regularly maintaining your home, learning basic DIY skills, shopping around for contractors, using quality materials, considering preventative measures, maintaining a home warranty, and taking advantage of tax credits, you can effectively save money on home maintenance and repairs. With patience, discipline, and a clear plan, you can achieve your home maintenance and repair goals and become a more financially savvy homeowner.

Chapter Seven

Planning for Emergencies and Unexpected Expenses

Emergencies and unexpected expenses can happen to anyone at any time. From medical bills to car repairs to unexpected home repairs, these expenses can quickly drain your savings and put you in a tough financial situation. However, by planning ahead and saving for emergencies, you can be better prepared for unexpected expenses and avoid financial stress. In this essay, we will discuss several strategies for planning for emergencies and unexpected expenses.

Build an emergency fund

Building an emergency fund is one of the most important steps you can take to prepare for unexpected expenses. Aim to save three to six months' worth of living expenses in an emergency fund. This can help you cover unexpected expenses, such as medical bills or car repairs, without having to rely on credit cards or loans.

Create a budget

Creating a budget can also help you prepare for unexpected expenses by giving you a better understanding of your income and expenses. By tracking your spending and setting aside money for savings each month, you can be better prepared for unexpected expenses when they arise.

Prioritize your expenses

Prioritizing your expenses can also help you prepare for unexpected expenses. Make a list of your essential expenses, such as housing, food, and utilities, and prioritize those expenses over non-essential expenses, such as entertainment or dining out. This can help you save money and build your emergency fund more quickly.

Consider insurance

Consider insurance as a way to protect yourself from unexpected expenses. Health insurance can help cover the cost of medical bills, while car insurance can help cover the cost of car repairs. Homeowners insurance can also help cover the cost of unexpected home repairs. Be sure to read your insurance policies carefully and understand what is and isn't covered.

Reduce debt

Reducing debt can also help you prepare for unexpected expenses by freeing up more money in your budget. Focus on paying off high-interest debt, such as credit card debt, first. This can help you save money on interest and free up more money for savings and emergencies.

Save for specific expenses

In addition to building an emergency fund, consider saving for specific expenses that you know are coming up. For example, if you know you will need a new car in the next few years, start saving for it now. This can help you avoid taking on debt to cover the cost of the expense.

Be flexible

Finally, be flexible when it comes to unexpected expenses. If you need to adjust your budget or dip into your emergency fund, don't beat yourself up about it. Unexpected expenses happen to everyone, and it's important to be able to adapt and make changes when necessary.

In conclusion, planning for emergencies and unexpected expenses is an important part of maintaining your financial health. By building an emergency fund, creating a budget, prioritizing your expenses, considering insurance, reducing debt, saving for specific expenses, and being flexible, you can be better prepared for unexpected expenses and avoid financial stress. With patience, discipline, and a clear plan, you can achieve your financial goals and become a more financially savvy individual.

Building an Emergency Fund

An emergency fund is an essential component of any financial plan. An emergency fund is a savings account that is specifically set aside for unexpected expenses, such as medical bills, car repairs, or home repairs. The purpose of an emergency fund is to provide a financial cushion and to prevent you from having to rely on credit cards or loans to cover unexpected expenses. In this essay, we will discuss several strategies for building an emergency fund.

Set a savings goal

The first step in building an emergency fund is to set a savings goal. Aim to save three to six months' worth of living expenses in an emergency fund. This can provide a financial cushion that can help you cover unexpected expenses without having to rely on credit cards or loans.

Create a budget

Creating a budget can also help you build an emergency fund. By tracking your income and expenses, you can identify areas where you can cut back on spending and redirect that money towards savings. Be sure to set aside a specific amount each month for your emergency fund.

Automate your savings

Automating your savings is another effective way to build an emergency fund. Set up automatic transfers from your checking account to your emergency fund each month. This can help you stay on track with your savings goal and make saving a habit.

Save windfalls

Saving windfalls, such as tax refunds or bonuses, is another effective way to build an emergency fund. Instead of spending the money, deposit it directly into your emergency fund. This can help you reach your savings goal more quickly.

Cut back on expenses

Cutting back on expenses is another effective way to build an emergency fund. Look for areas where you can reduce your spending, such as dining out or entertainment, and redirect that money towards savings. Small changes can add up over time and help you build your emergency fund more quickly.

Use cash windfalls

Using cash windfalls, such as inheritances or lottery winnings, to build an emergency fund is also a good strategy. While it may be tempting to spend the money on something fun or frivolous, depositing it directly into your emergency fund can help you prepare for unexpected expenses and provide peace of mind.

Avoid dipping into your emergency fund

Finally, it's important to avoid dipping into your emergency fund for non-emergency expenses. While it may be tempting to use the money for a vacation or a new car, this can set you back in your savings goals and leave you vulnerable to unexpected expenses.

In conclusion, building an emergency fund is an important part of any financial plan. By setting a savings goal, creating a budget, automating your savings, saving windfalls, cutting back on expenses, using cash windfalls, and avoiding dipping into your emergency fund, you can effectively build an emergency fund and prepare for unexpected expenses. With patience, discipline, and a clear plan, you can achieve your financial goals and become a more financially savvy individual.

Protecting Yourself with Insurance

Insurance is a way to protect yourself from financial loss in the event of unexpected events, such as illness, accidents, or natural disasters. While insurance can be an added expense, it can also provide peace of mind and prevent you from having to cover large expenses out of pocket. In this essay, we will discuss several types of insurance and how they can protect you and save you money in the long run.

Health insurance

Health insurance is one of the most important types of insurance you can have. It can help cover the cost of medical expenses, such as doctor visits, hospital stays, and prescription medications. Without health insurance, these expenses can quickly add up and put you in a tough financial situation. Be sure to review your health insurance policy carefully and understand what is and isn't covered.

Auto insurance

Auto insurance is another important type of insurance. In most states, it is mandatory to have auto insurance to drive a car legally. Auto insurance can help cover the cost of car repairs or medical expenses in the event of an accident. Be sure to review your auto insurance policy carefully and understand what is and isn't covered.

Homeowners or renters insurance

Homeowners or renters insurance can help protect your home and personal property from unexpected events, such as fires, theft, or natural disasters. Homeowners insurance can also cover the cost of unexpected repairs to your home. Be sure to review your homeowners or renters insurance policy carefully and understand what is and isn't covered.

Life insurance

Life insurance can provide financial support to your loved ones in the event of your unexpected death. It can help cover funeral expenses, outstanding debts, and other expenses your loved ones may face. Be sure to review your life insurance policy carefully and understand what is and isn't covered.

Disability insurance

Disability insurance can provide financial support if you become unable to work due to an illness or injury. It can help cover your living expenses, such as rent or mortgage payments, while you are unable to work. Be sure to review your disability insurance policy carefully and understand what is and isn't covered.

Liability insurance

Liability insurance can help protect you in the event that you are held responsible for damages or injuries to another person. For example, if you are involved in a car accident and are found to be at fault, liability insurance can help cover the cost of damages and medical expenses. Be sure to review your liability insurance policy carefully and understand what is and isn't covered.

In conclusion, insurance is an essential part of protecting yourself from financial loss in the event of unexpected events. By having the right types of insurance, such as health insurance, auto insurance, homeowners or renters insurance, life insurance, disability insurance, and liability insurance, you can protect yourself and save money in the long run. Be sure to review your insurance policies carefully and understand what is and isn't covered, and consider working with an insurance professional to help you select the best policies for your needs.

Preparing for Job Loss or Income Reduction

Losing your job or experiencing a reduction in income can be a stressful and challenging experience. However, there are steps you can take to prepare for the possibility of job loss or income reduction and mitigate the financial impact. In this essay, we will discuss several strategies for preparing for job loss or income reduction.

Build an emergency fund

An emergency fund is a savings account that is specifically set aside for unexpected expenses, such as medical bills, car repairs, or home repairs. The purpose of an emergency fund is to provide a financial cushion and to prevent you from having to rely on credit cards or loans to cover unexpected expenses. Aim to save three to six months' worth of living expenses in an emergency fund. This can provide a financial cushion that can help you cover unexpected expenses without having to rely on credit cards or loans.

Reduce your expenses

Reducing your expenses can also help you prepare for job loss or income reduction. Look for areas where you can cut back on spending, such as dining out or entertainment, and redirect that money towards savings. Small changes can add up over time and help you build your emergency fund more quickly.

Review your budget

Review your budget and identify areas where you can cut back on spending. Look for areas where you can reduce your expenses, such as dining out or entertainment, and redirect that money towards savings. Be sure to set aside a specific amount each month for your emergency fund.

Find ways to increase your income

Finding ways to increase your income can also help you prepare for job loss or income reduction. Consider taking on a part-time job or freelance work. You can also look for ways to monetize your hobbies or skills.

Network and develop new skills

Networking and developing new skills can also help you prepare for job loss or income reduction. Attend networking events, join professional organizations, and take courses or workshops to develop new skills. This can help you stay competitive in the job market and increase your chances of finding new employment.

Review your insurance policies

Review your insurance policies and understand what they cover. Make sure you have adequate health insurance, disability insurance, and life insurance. These can provide financial support in the event of unexpected events, such as illness or injury.

Create a plan

Creating a plan can help you prepare for job loss or income reduction. Identify your expenses and determine which ones are essential and which ones can be cut back. Develop a plan for how you will cover your essential expenses if you lose your job or experience a reduction in income.

In conclusion, preparing for job loss or income reduction is an essential part of any financial plan. By building an emergency fund, reducing your expenses, reviewing your budget, finding ways to increase your income, networking and developing new skills, reviewing your insurance policies, and creating a plan, you can effectively prepare for unexpected events and mitigate the financial impact. With patience, discipline, and a clear plan, you can achieve your financial goals and become a more financially savvy individual.

Chapter Eight

Saving on Entertainment and Leisure

Entertainment and leisure activities are an important part of life, but they can also be a significant expense. From going to the movies to traveling, the cost of entertainment and leisure can quickly add up. However, there are ways to enjoy these activities without breaking the bank. In this essay, we will discuss several strategies for saving money on entertainment and leisure.

Look for free activities

There are many free activities available that can provide entertainment and leisure without costing anything. For example, you can go for a hike, have a picnic in the park, or visit a museum on a free admission day. Check local listings or community bulletin boards for free events in your area.

Use coupons and discounts

Coupons and discounts can also help you save money on entertainment and leisure activities. Look for coupons or discount codes online for movies, concerts, or other events. Many credit cards also offer cash back or rewards for entertainment purchases, so be sure to check your credit card rewards program.

Plan ahead

Planning ahead can also help you save money on entertainment and leisure. For example, if you plan your vacation in advance, you may be able to take advantage of early booking discounts. If you plan to attend a concert or sporting event, buy your tickets early to take advantage of early bird pricing.

Share the cost

Sharing the cost of entertainment and leisure activities can also help you save money. For example, if you're planning a vacation with friends, consider splitting the cost of a rental home or hotel room. You can also split the cost of meals or tickets to events.

Use loyalty programs

Loyalty programs can also help you save money on entertainment and leisure activities. Many businesses, such as movie theaters, restaurants, and travel companies, offer loyalty programs that provide discounts or rewards for frequent customers. Be sure to sign up for these programs and take advantage of the rewards.

Opt for cheaper alternatives

Opting for cheaper alternatives can also help you save money on entertainment and leisure. For example, instead of going out to a fancy restaurant, have a potluck dinner with friends. Instead of going to a movie theater, have a movie night at home. Look for alternatives that can provide the same level of enjoyment without the high cost.

Set a budget

Setting a budget for entertainment and leisure can also help you save money. Determine how much you can afford to spend each month on these activities and stick to that budget. This will help you avoid overspending and ensure that you're not sacrificing your financial goals for entertainment.

In conclusion, entertainment and leisure are important parts of life, but they don't have to break the bank. By looking for free activities, using coupons and discounts, planning ahead, sharing the cost, using loyalty programs, opting for cheaper alternatives, and setting a budget, you can enjoy these activities without sacrificing your financial goals. With a little creativity and planning, you can have fun while still saving money.

Finding Affordable Hobbies and Activities

Hobbies and activities are an important part of life that can bring joy, fulfillment, and relaxation. However, they can also be a significant expense. From sports and fitness to arts and crafts, the cost of pursuing hobbies and activities can quickly add up. Fortunately, there are ways to find affordable hobbies and activities that can provide enjoyment without breaking the bank. In this essay, we will discuss several strategies for finding affordable hobbies and activities.

Explore low-cost options

One of the best ways to find affordable hobbies and activities is to explore low-cost options. For example, instead of joining an expensive gym, consider going for a run outside or doing a workout at home with free online videos. If you're interested in learning a new skill, check out local community centers, libraries, and adult education programs that offer affordable classes.

Use free resources

Many hobbies and activities can be enjoyed without spending any money at all. For example, if you enjoy reading, visit your local library instead of buying books. If you enjoy outdoor activities, go for a hike or take a bike ride. Look for free resources and activities that align with your interests.

Borrow or rent equipment

Purchasing equipment for hobbies and activities can be expensive, but you may not need to own everything yourself. Consider borrowing or renting equipment instead of buying it. For example, if you're interested in photography, borrow a camera from a friend or rent one from a camera rental store.

Look for discounts and deals

Just like with entertainment and leisure activities, look for discounts and deals when pursuing hobbies and activities. Many businesses offer discounts for first-time customers or for signing up for a subscription. Look for coupons or discount codes online, and sign up for email newsletters to stay informed about special offers.

Shop secondhand

Shopping secondhand can also help you save money on hobbies and activities. For example, if you enjoy playing music, look for used instruments online or at secondhand stores. If you're interested in art, look for used art supplies at thrift stores or online marketplaces.

Join a community group

Joining a community group can also help you find affordable hobbies and activities. Look for groups in your area that share your interests, such as a running club or a book club. These groups often organize free or low-cost activities and events, and can also provide a supportive community.

Start a hobby or activity with friends

Starting a hobby or activity with friends can also help you save money. For example, instead of hiring a personal trainer, work out with a friend. If you're interested in learning a new language, practice with a friend who speaks that language. Starting a hobby or activity with friends can also make it more enjoyable and provide a social aspect.

In conclusion, pursuing hobbies and activities doesn't have to be expensive. By exploring low-cost options, using free resources, borrowing or renting equipment, looking for discounts and deals, shopping secondhand, joining a community group, and starting a hobby or activity with friends, you can find affordable ways to enjoy your interests. Remember that the most important thing is to find hobbies and activities that bring you joy and fulfillment, regardless of the cost.

Saving Money on Dining Out and Socializing

Dining out and socializing are common activities that many people enjoy, but they can also be a significant expense. From restaurants and bars to concerts and events, the cost of socializing and dining out can quickly add up. However, there are several strategies for saving money on these activities without sacrificing fun and enjoyment. In this essay, we will discuss some tips for saving money on dining out and socializing.

Look for happy hour and specials

One of the best ways to save money on dining out and socializing is to look for happy hour and specials. Many restaurants and bars offer discounted drinks and food during specific hours or days of the week. Look for happy hour deals, discounted appetizers, and other specials that can help you save money while still enjoying a night out.

Use coupons and promo codes

Another way to save money on dining out and socializing is to use coupons and promo codes. Many restaurants and entertainment venues offer coupons or promo codes that can be found online or in local advertisements. Look for discounts on restaurant websites, apps, and social media pages, and sign up for email newsletters to stay informed about special offers.

Share meals and drinks

Sharing meals and drinks with friends can also help you save money while dining out and socializing. Splitting appetizers or entrees can reduce the cost of a meal, and sharing a pitcher of beer or a bottle of wine can be more cost-effective than buying individual drinks.

Eat before going out

Another way to save money on dining out is to eat a meal or snack before going out. This can help you avoid ordering too much food or drinks at the restaurant, and can also prevent you from being tempted to order expensive appetizers or desserts.

Host gatherings at home

Hosting gatherings at home can also be a great way to save money on socializing. Instead of going out to a restaurant or bar, invite friends over for a potluck dinner or game night. This can be a fun and affordable way to socialize while still enjoying good food and company.

Attend free events

Attending free events is another way to save money on socializing. Look for free concerts, festivals, and other events in your local community. These events can provide a fun and enjoyable social experience without costing you any money.

Set a budget

Setting a budget for dining out and socializing can also help you save money. Determine how much you can afford to spend on these activities each month, and stick to that budget. This can help you avoid overspending and can also help you prioritize which events and restaurants are most important to you.

In conclusion, dining out and socializing can be expensive, but there are several strategies for saving money on these activities. By looking for happy hour and specials, using coupons and promo codes, sharing meals and drinks, eating before going out, hosting gatherings at home, attending free events, and setting a budget, you can enjoy these activities without breaking the bank. Remember that the most important thing is to spend time with the people you care about and have fun, regardless of the cost.

Budget-Friendly Travel and Vacation Ideas

Traveling and taking vacations can be a great way to unwind, explore new places, and create lasting memories with loved ones. However, these experiences can often come with a high price tag. Fortunately, there are many budget-friendly travel and vacation ideas that can help you save money while still enjoying all the benefits of travel. In this essay, we will discuss some tips for planning a budget-friendly vacation.

Choose affordable destinations

Choosing affordable destinations is the first step in planning a budget-friendly vacation. Look for destinations that offer low-cost accommodations, dining, and activities. Consider traveling during the off-season, when prices for airfare and lodging may be lower. Additionally, look for destinations that offer free or low-cost attractions, such as museums, parks, and beaches.

Consider alternative accommodations

Hotels can be expensive, especially in popular tourist destinations. Consider alternative accommodations, such as vacation rentals, hostels, or camping. Vacation rentals can often be more affordable than hotels, especially for larger groups or longer stays. Hostels can offer low-cost lodging and a social atmosphere, and camping can provide an affordable and adventurous way to experience the outdoors.

Use budget airlines

Airfare can be a major expense when traveling. Look for budget airlines that offer lower fares than traditional airlines. While budget airlines may have additional fees for things like checked baggage and seat selection, they can still be a more affordable option for air travel.

Plan meals in advance

Eating out can be a significant expense when traveling. Plan meals in advance to save money on dining. Consider packing snacks or making sandwiches for lunches on the go. Look for restaurants that offer happy hour specials or early bird discounts, and consider cooking meals at your accommodations using local ingredients.

Take advantage of free activities

Many destinations offer free activities, such as hiking trails, parks, and beaches. Look for free events and attractions in the area you are visiting. Additionally, consider taking walking tours or exploring on your own to save money on expensive guided tours.

Look for discount passes and coupons

Many destinations offer discount passes that provide access to multiple attractions at a lower cost than purchasing individual tickets. Look for these passes online or at local tourist offices. Additionally, look for coupons and discounts for activities and restaurants in the area.

Use public transportation

Renting a car can be expensive, especially in cities where parking can be difficult or expensive. Consider using public transportation, such as buses or trains, to get around. Many cities offer day or weekly passes for public transportation that can save money compared to individual fares.

Consider a staycation

A staycation can be a great way to save money on travel while still enjoying time off. Consider exploring local attractions, museums, and parks. Look for discounted tickets or free admission days. Additionally, consider taking a break from technology and work during your staycation to truly unwind and relax.

In conclusion, budget-friendly travel and vacation ideas are a great way to save money while still enjoying all the benefits of travel. By choosing affordable destinations, considering alternative accommodations, using budget airlines, planning meals in advance, taking advantage of free activities, looking for discount passes and coupons, using public transportation, and considering a staycation, you can plan a memorable vacation without breaking the bank. Remember that the most important part of travel is the experience, not the cost.

Tips to help you save money on entertainment and leisure activities:

Chapter Nine

Investing in Your Future

- Look for free events in your community, such as concerts or festivals.
- Use coupons or discounts to save on movie tickets or rentals.
- Host a game night with friends instead of going out.
- Take advantage of free museum days or exhibits.
- Use a library to borrow books, movies, and music.
- Look for free or low-cost classes, such as fitness or dance classes.
- Use a streaming service instead of paying for cable TV.
- Attend a matinee movie instead of a prime time showing.
- Use a discount app or website to find deals on activities and events.
- Host a potluck dinner or BBQ instead of going out to eat.
- Use a free park or beach instead of paying for a resort or amusement park.
- Look for free or low-cost outdoor activities, such as hiking or biking.

- Use a community pool or beach instead of paying for a private pool or resort.
- Use a coupon or discount to save on a spa day or massage.
- Host a DIY craft night with friends instead of buying expensive crafts.
- Use a discount app or website to save on travel and hotel accommodations.
- Use a local community center for free or low-cost activities and events.
- Look for free or low-cost theater productions or plays.
- Attend a local sporting event instead of a professional one.
- Use a discount app or website to save on amusement park tickets.
- Host a book club or movie night with friends instead of going out.
- Look for free or low-cost art exhibits or galleries.
- Use a discount app or website to find deals on concerts and shows.
- Host a potluck game day with friends instead of going out.
- Look for free or low-cost outdoor concerts or music festivals.
- Use a discount app or website to save on sporting event tickets.
- Host a DIY home improvement or renovation project with friends.
- Use a discount app or website to save on theme park tickets.

- Look for free or low-cost comedy shows or open mic nights.
- Attend a free or low-cost community theater production.
- Host a DIY home decor or furniture building project with friends.
- Look for free or low-cost historical exhibits or tours.
- Use a discount app or website to save on water park tickets.
- Attend a free or low-cost nature hike or park tour.
- Host a DIY gardening or outdoor landscaping project with friends.
- Look for free or low-cost science exhibits or museums.
- Attend a free or low-cost community festival or fair.
- Use a discount app or website to save on ski resort tickets.
- Host a DIY cooking or baking project with friends.
- Look for free or low-cost cultural exhibits or museums.
- Attend a free or low-cost local theater production.
- Use a discount app or website to save on water sports or activities.
- Host a DIY art or painting project with friends.
- Look for free or low-cost holiday events or exhibits.
- Attend a free or low-cost local music or concert event.

- Use a discount app or website to save on snow sports or activities.
- Host a DIY fitness or wellness event with friends.
- Look for free or low-cost science or nature exhibits or tours.
- Attend a free or low-cost local art show or exhibit.
- Use a discount app or website to save on adventure sports or activities.

Investing in your future is an essential component of financial planning. Saving money and managing debt are important, but investing allows you to grow your wealth and achieve long-term financial goals. In this essay, we will discuss the benefits of investing in your future and some strategies for getting started.

Why Invest?

Investing is a way to grow your wealth over time. By putting your money into assets that have the potential to appreciate in value, you can earn a return on your investment. Over the long-term, this return can compound, allowing your money to grow exponentially.

Investing can also help you achieve your financial goals. Whether you are saving for retirement, a down payment on a home, or your child's education, investing can help you reach these goals faster than simply saving money in a bank account.

Additionally, investing can be a hedge against inflation. Inflation can erode the purchasing power of your savings over time. By investing in assets that have the potential to appreciate in value at a rate higher than inflation, you can protect your savings from the effects of inflation.

Getting Started with Investing

If you are new to investing, the prospect can be daunting. However, getting started is easier than you might think. Here are some strategies for getting started with investing:

Determine your goals

Before you begin investing, it is important to determine your goals. What are you saving for? How much money do you need to achieve these goals? What is your time horizon for achieving these goals? Once you have a clear understanding of your goals, you can begin to develop an investment strategy that will help you achieve them.

Develop a diversified portfolio

Diversification is an important aspect of investing. By investing in a variety of assets, you can spread your risk and reduce the impact of market volatility on your portfolio. A diversified portfolio should include a mix of stocks, bonds, and other assets that are appropriate for your goals, risk tolerance, and time horizon.

Consider your risk tolerance

Your risk tolerance is an important factor to consider when investing. Generally, the higher the potential return of an investment, the higher the risk. It is important to consider your risk tolerance when developing your investment strategy. If you are uncomfortable with the level of risk in your portfolio, it may be necessary to adjust your investments to better align with your risk tolerance.

Start small

You do not need to have a lot of money to start investing. Many brokerage firms allow you to open an account with a small amount of money. Additionally, some robo-advisors offer low-cost investment options that are ideal for those just starting out.

Keep costs low

Investing can be expensive, especially if you are paying high fees for investment products. It is important to keep your investment costs low to maximize your returns. Look for low-cost investment options, such as index funds or ETFs, and avoid high-cost investment products, such as actively managed mutual funds.

Stay disciplined

Investing requires discipline and patience. It is important to stay disciplined and avoid making emotional decisions based on short-term market fluctuations. Stick to your investment strategy, and avoid making changes based on market volatility.

Conclusion

Investing in your future is an important aspect of financial planning. It allows you to grow your wealth over time, achieve your financial goals, and protect your savings from inflation. By developing a diversified portfolio, considering your risk tolerance, starting small, keeping costs low, and staying disciplined, you can begin to build a solid foundation for your financial future. Remember, investing is a long-term strategy, and it is important to stay focused on your goals and avoid making emotional decisions based on short-term market fluctuations.

Understanding Different Investment Options

Investing your money can be a great way to build wealth over time. However, with so many investment options available, it can be overwhelming to determine where to invest your money. In this essay, we will discuss some of the most common investment options and their potential risks and benefits.

Stocks

Stocks are ownership shares in a company. When you buy a stock, you are buying a small piece of ownership in that company. Stocks can offer the potential for high returns, but they also carry significant risk. Stock prices can fluctuate rapidly based on market conditions, and it is possible to lose all of your investment if the company goes bankrupt.

Bonds

Bonds are debt securities issued by companies or governments. When you buy a bond, you are essentially loaning money to the issuer. In exchange, the issuer pays you interest over a set period of time. Bonds are generally considered to be lower risk than stocks, but they also offer lower returns. Additionally, bond prices can be affected by changes in interest rates.

Mutual Funds

Mutual funds are investment vehicles that pool money from many investors to purchase a diversified portfolio of stocks, bonds, or other assets. Mutual funds can offer diversification and professional management, but they also carry fees and expenses that can eat into your returns.

Exchange-Traded Funds (ETFs)

ETFs are similar to mutual funds in that they pool money from many investors to purchase a diversified portfolio of assets. However, ETFs trade on an exchange like a stock, and their prices can fluctuate throughout the day. ETFs can offer diversification and low costs, but they also carry risks similar to those of mutual funds.

Real Estate

Real estate can be a great long-term investment option. It offers the potential for rental income and capital appreciation. However, real estate also requires significant upfront costs and ongoing maintenance expenses. Additionally, real estate prices can be affected by changes in the local housing market.

Commodities

Commodities are physical goods such as gold, oil, and wheat. Investing in commodities can offer diversification and protection against inflation, but it also carries significant risks. Commodity prices can be volatile, and there are no guarantees of returns.

Cryptocurrencies

Cryptocurrencies such as Bitcoin and Ethereum are digital currencies that operate independently of a central bank. Investing in cryptocurrencies can offer the potential for high returns, but it also carries significant risk. Cryptocurrency prices can be highly volatile, and there is no guarantee of returns.

Conclusion

Understanding the different investment options available is an important aspect of financial planning. Each investment option has its own potential risks and benefits, and it is important to consider your goals, risk tolerance, and time horizon when choosing where to invest your money. Diversification is also an important consideration, as it can help spread your risk and reduce the impact of market volatility on your portfolio. Remember, investing is a long-term strategy, and it is important to stay focused on your goals and avoid making emotional decisions based on short-term market fluctuations. By developing a diversified portfolio and staying disciplined, you can begin to build a solid foundation for your financial future.

Saving for Retirement

Saving for retirement is a crucial aspect of financial planning that many people tend to overlook. While it can be tempting to focus on immediate expenses and lifestyle choices, planning for retirement should be a top priority for anyone who wants to achieve long-term financial security. In this essay, we will discuss some strategies for saving for retirement and the benefits of starting early.

Start Early

One of the most important strategies for saving for retirement is to start early. The earlier you start saving, the more time your money has to grow. For example, if you start saving at age 25 and contribute $5,000 per year to a retirement account with an average annual return of 7%, you could have over $1 million by age 65. However, if you wait until age 35 to start saving, you would need to contribute over $10,000 per year to achieve the same result.

Contribute to a Retirement Account

One of the most common ways to save for retirement is to contribute to a retirement account such as a 401(k) or IRA. These accounts offer tax benefits and can be an effective way to save for retirement. For example, if you contribute to a traditional 401(k) or IRA, your contributions are tax-deductible, which can lower your taxable income and reduce your tax bill. Additionally, your investments grow tax-free until you withdraw them in retirement.

Take Advantage of Employer Matches

If your employer offers a 401(k) or other retirement plan, it is important to take advantage of any matching contributions they offer. Many employers will match a certain percentage of your contributions, which can significantly increase your retirement savings. For example, if your employer matches 50% of your contributions up to 6% of your salary, and you earn $50,000 per year, you could receive an additional $1,500 per year in retirement savings just from employer matches.

Consider a Roth IRA

Another option for retirement savings is a Roth IRA. Unlike traditional retirement accounts, contributions to a Roth IRA are made with after-tax dollars. However, your investments grow tax-free and withdrawals in retirement are also tax-free. This can be a good option for people who expect to be in a higher tax bracket in retirement than they are currently.

Automate Your Savings

One way to make sure you are consistently saving for retirement is to automate your savings. This means setting up automatic contributions to your retirement account each month. By doing this, you can ensure that you are saving regularly and avoid the temptation to spend the money on other expenses.

Be Consistent

Consistency is key when it comes to saving for retirement. It is important to set a realistic savings goal and stick to it. Even small contributions can add up over time, so it is better to save consistently than to try to make up for lost time later on.

Review Your Investments Regularly

It is also important to regularly review your retirement investments to ensure they are aligned with your goals and risk tolerance. As you get closer to retirement age, you may want to adjust your investments to be more conservative and focus on preserving your savings rather than growth.

Conclusion

Saving for retirement is an essential part of financial planning that requires discipline, consistency, and a long-term mindset. By starting early, contributing to retirement accounts, taking advantage of employer matches, considering Roth IRAs, automating your savings, being consistent, and reviewing your investments regularly, you can build a solid foundation for your retirement years. Remember, the earlier you start saving, the more time your money has to grow, so don't delay in taking action to secure your financial future.

Investing in Real Estate and Other Assets

Investing in real estate and other assets can be a great way to grow your wealth and achieve financial security. However, it is important to understand the risks and benefits of different types of investments before making any decisions. In this essay, we will discuss some strategies for investing in real estate and other assets and the potential benefits they can offer.

Real Estate Investments

Real estate can be a great investment for long-term wealth building. One of the primary benefits of real estate is its potential for passive income. By purchasing rental properties, you can generate rental income that can provide a steady stream of cash flow. Real estate also tends to appreciate in value over time, providing an opportunity for long-term capital appreciation.

There are several different ways to invest in real estate, including:

1. Rental Properties: Purchasing rental properties can be a great way to generate passive income. However, it is important to carefully consider the costs and risks associated with property management, including repairs, vacancies, and tenant turnover.

2. Real Estate Investment Trusts (REITs): REITs are companies that own and manage income-generating real estate properties. By investing in REITs, you can gain exposure to the real estate market without the hassle of managing properties.

3. Real Estate Crowdfunding: Real estate crowdfunding platforms allow individual investors to pool their money together to invest in real estate projects. This can be a good option for investors who want to invest in real estate but don't have the capital to purchase a property on their own.

Stocks and Bonds

Stocks and bonds are another common type of investment that can offer the potential for long-term growth. Stocks represent ownership in a company and can provide capital appreciation as the company grows and profits increase. Bonds, on the other hand, represent a loan to a company or government and provide fixed income through interest payments.

There are several different types of stocks and bonds to consider, including:

4. Index Funds: Index funds are mutual funds or exchange-traded funds (ETFs) that track a specific market index, such as the S&P 500. By investing in index funds, you can gain exposure to the broader market and benefit from long-term market growth.

5. Dividend Stocks: Dividend stocks are stocks that pay out a portion of their earnings to shareholders in the form of dividends. This can provide a steady stream of passive income for investors.

6. Corporate Bonds: Corporate bonds are debt securities issued by companies to raise capital. They typically offer higher yields than government bonds but come with higher risks.

Alternative Investments

In addition to real estate and traditional investments, there are also a variety of alternative investments to consider. These can include:

7. Private Equity: Private equity investments involve investing in private companies that are not publicly traded. This can provide an opportunity for high returns, but also comes with higher risks.

8. Commodities: Commodities such as gold, silver, and oil can provide a hedge against inflation and market volatility.

9. Cryptocurrencies: Cryptocurrencies such as Bitcoin and Ethereum have gained popularity in recent years as a high-risk, high-reward investment option.

Diversification

Regardless of the type of investment you choose, it is important to diversify your portfolio to minimize risk. This means investing in a variety of assets across different sectors and industries. By diversifying your portfolio, you can reduce your exposure to any one particular asset class or company and reduce your overall risk.

Conclusion

Investing in real estate and other assets can be a great way to grow your wealth and achieve financial security. By considering different types of investments, including real estate, stocks and bonds, and alternative investments, you can build a diversified portfolio that can weather market volatility and provide long-term growth.

Chapter Ten

Saving for Education

Education is a valuable asset that can bring about numerous opportunities for personal and professional growth. However, it can be expensive, and not everyone can afford to pay for it out of pocket. That's where saving for education comes in. In this essay, we will discuss the importance of saving for education, various ways to save for it, and some tips for getting started.

Importance of Saving for Education

Saving for education is important because it can help you avoid debt and achieve your educational goals. With the increasing cost of education, student loans are becoming more and more common. These loans can have a significant impact on a person's financial well-being, especially if they are unable to repay them. By saving for education, you can reduce the amount of debt you need to take on and decrease the burden of repaying it.

In addition, saving for education can provide you with more options when it comes to choosing the right educational institution or program. It can also give you the flexibility to take advantage of other opportunities such as studying abroad, pursuing internships or apprenticeships, or even starting your own business.

Ways to Save for Education

There are several ways to save for education, and the best option depends on your individual circumstances and goals. Here are some of the most common ways to save for education:

1. 529 plans: A 529 plan is a tax-advantaged savings plan designed specifically for education. It allows you to save money for qualified education expenses, such as tuition, fees, books, and room and board. The contributions to a 529 plan are made with after-tax dollars, but the earnings grow tax-free, and withdrawals for qualified expenses are also tax-free.

2. Coverdell Education Savings Account: A Coverdell Education Savings Account (ESA) is a tax-advantaged savings account that can be used to pay for qualified education expenses. It is similar to a 529 plan, but it has some key differences. For example, the contribution limits are lower, and the funds can be used for K-12 expenses in addition to higher education.

3. UGMA/UTMA accounts: UGMA (Uniform Gifts to Minors Act) and UTMA (Uniform Transfers to Minors Act) accounts are custodial accounts that allow you to save money for a child's education. The funds in these accounts can be used for any expense that benefits the child, including education. Once the child reaches the age of majority, the funds become the child's property and can be used for any purpose.

4. Roth IRA: A Roth IRA is a retirement savings account that allows you to withdraw your contributions tax-free at any time. While the primary purpose of a Roth IRA is retirement savings, you can also use the funds to pay for qualified education expenses without incurring a penalty.

Tips for Getting Started

Saving for education can be daunting, but it's important to start as early as possible. Here are some tips for getting started:

5. Set a savings goal: Determine how much you need to save for education and set a specific goal. This will help you stay motivated and track your progress.

6. Create a budget: Create a budget that includes your income and expenses, and allocate a portion of your income towards education savings.

7. Automate your savings: Set up automatic transfers from your checking account to your education savings account to make saving easier.

8. Consider a high-yield savings account: Look for a savings account with a high-interest rate to maximize your savings.

9. Explore financial aid options: Research financial aid options, such as scholarships, grants, and student loans, to determine what assistance may be available to you.

Planning for Your Children's Education

Planning for Your Children's Education

As a parent, one of your biggest financial concerns is likely to be your child's education. Education is expensive, and costs are rising every year. Whether your child is still in diapers or already in high school, it is never too early or too late to start planning for their education. In this essay, we will discuss some strategies for planning and saving for your children's education.

The first step in planning for your children's education is to set a goal. How much money do you want to save for each child's education, and when do you want to reach that goal? Start by researching the current cost of tuition, room and board, and other expenses at the schools your child is interested in attending. Keep in mind that these costs are likely to increase by the time your child is ready for college, so it is better to overestimate than to underestimate.

1. Once you have set your savings goal, it is time to start saving. One of the most popular ways to save for education is through a 529 college savings plan. These plans offer tax-free growth and withdrawals for qualified education expenses. There are two types of 529 plans: prepaid tuition plans and education savings plans. Prepaid tuition plans allow you to prepay tuition at today's prices for use in the future, while education savings plans allow you to invest in mutual funds or other investment options. The specific details of each plan can vary depending on the state, so be sure to research the options available to you.

Another option for saving for education is a Coverdell Education Savings Account (ESA). These accounts allow you to contribute up to $2,000 per year per child, and earnings are tax-free if used for qualified education expenses. Unlike 529 plans, Coverdell ESAs can be used for K-12 education expenses in addition to college expenses. However, income limits apply, and contributions are not tax-deductible.

If you are interested in more flexibility and control over your investments, you may consider a regular investment account. While this option does not offer the tax advantages of a 529 plan or ESA, it does give you more control over your investments and allows you to use the money for any purpose, including education expenses. Keep in mind, however, that any capital gains or dividends earned will be subject to taxes.

In addition to saving in a dedicated education account, you can also look for ways to reduce education costs. One way to do this is to encourage your child to apply for scholarships and grants. Many colleges and universities offer scholarships and grants based on academic achievement, extracurricular activities, and other factors. Encourage your child to start researching and applying for scholarships as early as possible.

Another way to reduce education costs is to consider community college or vocational school as an alternative to a four-year university. These schools offer many of the same programs and certifications at a fraction of the cost. Additionally, your child can transfer to a four-year university after completing their degree at a community college or vocational school.

Finally, consider starting a college fund for your child's education. This can be as simple as setting up a savings account and adding a little money each month. By starting early and making regular contributions, you can help ensure that your child has the financial resources they need to achieve their educational goals.

In conclusion, planning and saving for your children's education can seem overwhelming, but it is important to start early and have a plan. Consider your savings goals, research the options available to you, and look for ways to reduce education costs. With a little effort and planning, you can help ensure that your child has the financial resources they need to succeed in their educational pursuits.

Finding Scholarships and Grants

In today's world, a college education is a necessity for many people in order to succeed in their chosen careers. However, the cost of tuition, fees, books, and other expenses can be a major barrier for many individuals. Fortunately, there are many options available to help offset the cost of higher education, including scholarships and grants.

Scholarships and grants are both forms of financial aid that do not have to be repaid. However, they differ in how they are awarded and the requirements for eligibility.

Scholarships are typically awarded based on academic or athletic achievement, financial need, or a combination of both. Many scholarships are sponsored by private organizations, such as corporations, foundations, or community groups. Some are also offered by colleges and universities themselves. To be considered for a scholarship, students usually have to submit an application, which may require essays, letters of recommendation, and transcripts.

Grants, on the other hand, are typically awarded based on financial need. They may come from federal or state government programs, private foundations, or colleges and universities. To be eligible for a grant, students must submit a Free Application for Federal Student Aid (FAFSA) form, which takes into account their family's income and other financial factors.

In addition to scholarships and grants, there are other sources of financial aid available to students. These include work-study programs, which provide part-time jobs to students to help pay for their education, and loans, which must be repaid with interest after graduation.

One of the best ways to find scholarships and grants is to start early and be proactive. High school students should begin researching scholarship opportunities during their junior year, and should continue to search for and apply for scholarships throughout their senior year and during their college years.

There are many online resources available to help students find scholarships and grants, including websites such as Fastweb, Scholarships.com, and the College Board's Big Future. These sites allow students to search for scholarships based on their interests, background, and other factors.

Students can also check with their high school guidance counselor, college financial aid office, or local community organizations to find out about available scholarships and grants. Many organizations, such as religious groups, professional associations, and fraternal organizations, offer scholarships to their members or to students in their communities.

When applying for scholarships and grants, it's important to read the requirements carefully and follow all instructions. Students should make sure they are eligible for the award before applying, and should provide all necessary documentation and information. It's also a good idea to apply for as many scholarships as possible, since the competition for funding can be fierce.

In addition to scholarships and grants, there are other ways to save money on higher education. For example, attending a community college for the first two years of a four-year degree program can be a cost-effective way to earn a degree. Students can also save money by living at home, attending a school in-state, or choosing a less expensive college or university.

Overall, the key to finding financial aid for education is to start early, be proactive, and apply for as many scholarships and grants as possible. With careful planning and research, students can find the funding they need to pursue their academic and career goals without taking on excessive debt.

Reducing Student Loan Debt

Reducing student loan debt is an important financial goal for many individuals who have borrowed money to pay for their education. With the rising cost of tuition and fees, it can be challenging to avoid accruing a significant amount of student loan debt. However, there are various strategies that students and graduates can use to minimize the amount of debt they take on and pay it off more quickly. In this essay, we will explore several effective ways to reduce student loan debt.

One of the most effective strategies for reducing student loan debt is to minimize borrowing in the first place. This can be accomplished by carefully considering the cost of attendance and identifying ways to reduce expenses. Students can research and apply for scholarships, grants, and other forms of financial aid to offset the cost of tuition and fees. They can also look for opportunities to work part-time or take on internships that offer compensation or academic credit.

Another approach to minimizing student loan debt is to attend a lower-cost school or pursue alternative forms of education, such as vocational or trade schools, that offer affordable and practical training. These options can provide valuable skills and credentials while avoiding the high cost of a traditional four-year degree.

For those who have already incurred student loan debt, there are several strategies for reducing the amount owed and paying it off more quickly. One approach is to make extra payments on the principal balance of the loan. By doing so, borrowers can reduce the overall interest they will pay over the life of the loan and shorten the repayment period. Another effective strategy is to refinance student loans at a lower interest rate. This can help reduce monthly payments and make it easier to pay off debt more quickly.

Borrowers can also consider income-driven repayment plans, which base monthly payments on income and family size. These plans can be particularly helpful for those who have low income or high levels of debt relative to their income. In addition, borrowers can take advantage of loan forgiveness programs, such as Public Service Loan Forgiveness, which offers debt relief for those who work in certain public service jobs.

To further reduce student loan debt, borrowers can also look for ways to increase their income. This can include taking on additional work or seeking promotions or higher-paying jobs. They can also explore alternative sources of income, such as freelance work or starting a side business. By increasing their income, borrowers can not only reduce their student loan debt more quickly but also improve their overall financial situation.

In conclusion, reducing student loan debt is a crucial financial goal for many individuals. By minimizing borrowing, attending lower-cost schools, and pursuing alternative forms of education, students can avoid accruing significant debt. For those who have already incurred debt, strategies such as making extra payments, refinancing, and enrolling in income-driven repayment plans can help reduce the amount owed and shorten the repayment period. In addition, increasing income through additional work or alternative sources can further accelerate the process of paying off student loan debt. By implementing these strategies and taking a proactive approach to managing their finances, individuals can achieve financial security and independence in the years ahead.

Chapter Eleven

Saving on Healthcare Costs

Saving on Healthcare Costs

Healthcare costs can be a significant expense for many individuals and families, especially those with chronic medical conditions or large families. Fortunately, there are many ways to save money on healthcare costs without sacrificing the quality of care. This article will discuss some practical strategies to reduce healthcare costs and help you save money.

Take Advantage of Preventive Care

Prevention is the key to keeping healthcare costs under control. Many insurance plans cover preventive care services such as annual physical exams, vaccinations, and cancer screenings at no cost to the patient. Taking advantage of these services can help catch health issues early when they are easier and less expensive to treat. In addition, maintaining a healthy lifestyle through regular exercise and a balanced diet can also help prevent the onset of chronic diseases such as diabetes and heart disease, which can be expensive to manage.

Shop Around for Healthcare Services

Just like shopping around for other goods and services, it is important to compare prices and services for healthcare. The cost of medical services can vary widely among different providers, so it pays to do your research. You can start by checking with your insurance company to find out which providers are in-network and which services are covered. You can also check online for pricing information and read reviews from other patients. Some providers may offer discounts for cash payments or provide financing options to help you pay for your medical expenses over time.

Use Generic Drugs

Prescription drugs can be a significant expense for those with chronic medical conditions. However, using generic drugs instead of brand-name drugs can save you a considerable amount of money. Generic drugs are just as effective as their brand-name counterparts but are significantly less expensive. In addition, some pharmacies offer discount programs and coupons for generic drugs that can provide additional savings.

Consider Telemedicine

Telemedicine is an excellent option for those who live in remote areas or have difficulty traveling to a healthcare provider's office. With telemedicine, patients can receive medical care from the comfort of their own homes through video consultations with licensed healthcare providers. Telemedicine is often less expensive than in-person visits and can be a more convenient option for many patients.

Use Health Savings Accounts (HSAs)

Health Savings Accounts (HSAs) are a type of savings account that can be used to pay for healthcare expenses. HSAs are available to those who have a high-deductible health plan and can be used to pay for medical expenses such as deductibles, copayments, and prescription drugs. The contributions to an HSA are tax-deductible, and any funds left in the account at the end of the year can be carried over to the next year. HSAs are a great way to save money on healthcare costs while also taking advantage of tax benefits.

Negotiate Your Medical Bills

If you receive a medical bill that is more than you can afford, don't be afraid to negotiate. You can start by asking for an itemized bill to ensure that you are not being charged for services that you did not receive. You can also contact the billing department to ask about payment plans or discounts for paying in cash. In addition, you can seek assistance from nonprofit organizations that can help negotiate your medical bills on your behalf.

Take Advantage of Employer-Sponsored Benefits

Many employers offer healthcare benefits to their employees, including health insurance plans, wellness programs, and employee assistance programs (EAPs). These benefits can help you save money on healthcare costs and improve your overall well-being. Be sure to review your employer's benefit offerings and take advantage of any that can help you save money.

Choosing the Right Health Insurance Plan

Choosing the Right Health Insurance Plan

Health insurance is a necessary expense for most people, but the cost of premiums and deductibles can add up quickly. Choosing the right health insurance plan can help you save money on your healthcare costs while still receiving the care you need. In this essay, we will discuss the factors you should consider when choosing a health insurance plan and how to find the plan that is right for you.

Types of Health Insurance Plans

There are several types of health insurance plans to choose from, including Health Maintenance Organization (HMO), Preferred Provider Organization (PPO), Point of Service (POS), and High Deductible Health Plan (HDHP) with Health Savings Account (HSA).

HMO plans typically have lower premiums but require you to choose a primary care physician who coordinates your care and refers you to specialists as needed. PPO plans offer more flexibility in choosing providers but often come with higher premiums and out-of-pocket costs. POS plans are a combination of HMO and PPO plans, giving you the choice between in-network or out-of-network care. HDHPs are designed to keep monthly premiums low, but come with high deductibles and out-of-pocket costs. An HSA can be used to save money pre-tax to pay for medical expenses.

Factors to Consider

When choosing a health insurance plan, it's important to consider your healthcare needs and your budget. Here are some factors to consider:

1. Premiums: The amount you pay for your insurance plan each month.

2. Deductibles: The amount you pay out-of-pocket before your insurance coverage kicks in.

3. Copayments: The amount you pay each time you see a healthcare provider.

4. Coinsurance: The percentage of costs you are responsible for after you've met your deductible.

5. Maximum out-of-pocket costs: The most you will have to pay out-of-pocket in a year for covered medical expenses.

6. Network: The healthcare providers and facilities that are covered by your insurance plan.

7. Prescription drug coverage: The medications that are covered by your insurance plan and the cost.

8. Additional benefits: The extra services that are covered by your insurance plan, such as dental, vision, or mental health.

How to Find the Right Plan

To find the right health insurance plan, start by assessing your healthcare needs and budget. Consider how often you go to the doctor, whether you take prescription medications, and whether you have any ongoing medical conditions. Think about how much you can afford to spend on premiums, deductibles, and other out-of-pocket costs.

Next, research different health insurance plans and compare their costs and benefits. Many employers offer health insurance plans to their employees, so check with your employer first to see if you have this option. If you are self-employed or do not have access to health insurance through your employer, you can look for plans on the Health Insurance Marketplace or through a private insurance broker.

When comparing plans, make sure to read the plan details carefully, including the covered benefits, the network of healthcare providers, and the costs associated with the plan. Consider your healthcare needs and budget when choosing a plan, and don't be afraid to ask questions or seek help from a healthcare professional or insurance broker.

In addition, it's important to review your health insurance plan regularly to ensure it still meets your healthcare needs and budget. Changes in your healthcare needs or financial situation may require a change in your health insurance plan.

Conclusion

Choosing the right health insurance plan is an important decision that can have a significant impact on your healthcare costs and overall well-being. By considering your healthcare needs and budget, researching different plans, and comparing their costs and benefits, you can find the plan that is right for you. Remember to review your plan regularly to ensure it still meets your needs and budget.

Utilizing Preventive Care and Wellness Programs

Utilizing Preventive Care and Wellness Programs

Preventive care and wellness programs can help you stay healthy, catch health problems early, and save money on healthcare costs. Many health insurance plans now offer free preventive care services, such as annual check-ups and screenings for cancer, high blood pressure, and other conditions. Additionally, wellness programs can provide incentives for healthy behaviors, such as exercise, healthy eating, and smoking cessation. In this essay, we will explore the benefits of preventive care and wellness programs, and provide tips for utilizing them to save money on healthcare costs.

The Benefits of Preventive Care

Preventive care can help catch health problems early, when they are easier and less expensive to treat. For example, a routine mammogram can detect breast cancer before symptoms appear, making it easier to treat and potentially saving your life. Similarly, routine blood pressure screenings can catch high blood pressure before it causes serious health problems, such as heart attack or stroke. By catching health problems early, preventive care can help you avoid costly medical procedures and hospitalizations.

Preventive care can also help you maintain good health and prevent health problems from developing in the first place. Regular check-ups with your doctor can help you identify and address risk factors for chronic diseases, such as high blood pressure, high cholesterol, and diabetes. Additionally, preventive care services, such as immunizations and flu shots, can protect you from infectious diseases and prevent the spread of disease in your community.

The Benefits of Wellness Programs

Wellness programs can help you develop and maintain healthy habits that can prevent or manage chronic diseases. Many wellness programs provide incentives for healthy behaviors, such as exercise, healthy eating, and smoking cessation. For example, some health insurance plans offer discounts on gym memberships or reimbursements for fitness classes. Similarly, some wellness programs offer rewards for completing health assessments, participating in health coaching, or achieving certain health goals.

In addition to saving money on healthcare costs, wellness programs can also improve your overall health and well-being. Regular exercise and healthy eating can reduce your risk of chronic diseases, such as diabetes, heart disease, and cancer. Similarly, quitting smoking can improve your lung function and reduce your risk of lung cancer and other smoking-related illnesses.

Tips for Utilizing Preventive Care and Wellness Programs

To make the most of your preventive care and wellness programs, consider the following tips:

Know what services are covered by your health insurance plan. Many health insurance plans now offer free preventive care services, such as annual check-ups and screenings for cancer, high blood pressure, and other conditions. Additionally, many plans offer wellness programs that provide incentives for healthy behaviors, such as exercise, healthy eating, and smoking cessation.

Take advantage of free preventive care services. If your health insurance plan covers preventive care services, make sure to schedule regular check-ups and screenings. These services can help catch health problems early and prevent chronic diseases from developing.

Participate in wellness programs. If your health insurance plan offers a wellness program, consider participating. Many programs offer incentives for healthy behaviors, such as exercise, healthy eating, and smoking cessation.

Set health goals and track your progress. Setting health goals can help motivate you to adopt healthy habits and stick to them. Consider setting goals for exercise, healthy eating, smoking cessation, or other health behaviors, and track your progress using a fitness tracker, journal, or app.

Take advantage of community resources. Many communities offer free or low-cost resources for healthy living, such as walking trails, fitness classes, and farmers' markets. Consider taking advantage of these resources to support your healthy lifestyle.

Saving Money on Prescriptions and Medical Supplies

Saving money on prescriptions and medical supplies can be a daunting task for many people. However, there are ways to reduce these costs and save money while still receiving the necessary medical care. In this essay, we will explore some effective strategies for saving money on prescriptions and medical supplies.

1. Ask for Generic Brands: The first and most effective way to save money on prescriptions is to ask for generic brands. Generic drugs contain the

same active ingredients as their brand-name counterparts but are much less expensive. According to the FDA, generic drugs are required to be just as safe and effective as brand-name drugs. Therefore, it is recommended that you ask your doctor or pharmacist for a generic version of your prescribed medication.

2. Compare Prices: Prices for medications can vary widely between different pharmacies, so it is important to shop around and compare prices. You can use websites and apps such as GoodRx to compare prices and find the lowest cost for your medications. Some pharmacies also offer discount programs, so be sure to ask about these as well.

3. Utilize Prescription Discount Cards: Prescription discount cards are another way to save money on prescriptions. These cards are available through various organizations and offer discounts on prescription medications. You can find prescription discount cards online, and some pharmacies also offer their own discount cards.

4. Consider Mail-Order Pharmacies: Mail-order pharmacies can offer significant savings on prescription medications. These pharmacies often offer lower prices and can deliver your medication right to your door. Some insurance plans also offer discounts for using a mail-order pharmacy, so be sure to check with your insurance provider.

5. Use Patient Assistance Programs: Many pharmaceutical companies offer patient assistance programs for those who cannot afford their medications. These programs can provide free or discounted medications to those who qualify. You can find information about these programs on the pharmaceutical company's website or by speaking with your doctor or pharmacist.

6. Check with Your Insurance Provider: Be sure to check with your insurance provider to see if they offer any discounts or programs for prescription medications. Some insurance plans offer discounts for using certain

pharmacies or mail-order pharmacies, while others offer co-pay assistance programs.

7. Consider Over-the-Counter Options: In some cases, over-the-counter medications may be a viable alternative to prescription medications. Over-the-counter medications are often less expensive and can be just as effective for treating certain conditions. Be sure to speak with your doctor or pharmacist before using any over-the-counter medications.

8. Buy Medical Supplies in Bulk: If you use medical supplies such as bandages, gloves, or syringes, consider buying them in bulk. Buying in bulk can often save you money in the long run. You can find bulk medical supplies online or at medical supply stores.

9. Check with Your Insurance Provider for Medical Supply Coverage: Some insurance plans cover the cost of medical supplies such as diabetic testing supplies or durable medical equipment. Be sure to check with your insurance provider to see if you have any coverage for these items.

10. Utilize Medical Supply Exchange Programs: Medical supply exchange programs allow individuals to donate or exchange medical supplies with others. These programs can be a great way to obtain medical supplies for free or at a reduced cost.

In conclusion, there are many effective strategies for saving money on prescriptions and medical supplies. By following these tips, you can reduce your healthcare costs and still receive the necessary medical care. Remember to always speak with your doctor or pharmacist before making any changes to your medication or treatment plan.

Chapter Twelve

Tax Planning and Saving Strategies

Tax planning is an essential part of personal finance management that can help you save money in the long run. Whether you are a student, a working professional, or a retiree, understanding tax laws and regulations can significantly impact your financial well-being. In this essay, we will discuss tax planning and saving strategies that can help you maximize your income and reduce your tax liability.

1. Understand the tax laws and regulations: The first step to effective tax planning is to have a thorough understanding of tax laws and regulations. This includes knowing the tax brackets, deductions, credits, and exemptions that apply to your income level and circumstances. You can consult with a tax professional or use tax software to help you understand the tax code and how it applies to you.

2. Take advantage of tax-deferred retirement accounts: One of the most effective tax-saving strategies is to contribute to tax-deferred retirement accounts such as 401(k) and IRA accounts. These accounts allow you to save money on a pre-tax basis, which means that you do not pay taxes on the money you contribute until you withdraw it in retirement. By reducing your taxable income, you can lower your tax liability and save money in the long run.

3. Consider itemizing your deductions: Itemizing your deductions can be an effective tax-saving strategy if you have significant expenses that qualify

for deductions. This includes expenses such as mortgage interest, property taxes, medical expenses, and charitable donations. By itemizing your deductions, you can reduce your taxable income and potentially lower your tax liability.

4. Make use of tax credits: Tax credits are a form of tax relief that directly reduces your tax liability. Common tax credits include the Earned Income Tax Credit, the Child Tax Credit, and the American Opportunity Tax Credit. By taking advantage of tax credits, you can reduce the amount of taxes you owe and potentially increase your refund.

5. Invest in tax-efficient investments: Investing in tax-efficient investments such as municipal bonds, index funds, and exchange-traded funds (ETFs) can help you save money on taxes. These investments are structured in a way that minimizes the tax burden on investors, allowing you to keep more of your earnings.

6. Take advantage of employer benefits: Many employers offer benefits that can help you save money on taxes. This includes programs such as flexible spending accounts (FSAs), health savings accounts (HSAs), and commuter benefits. By making use of these benefits, you can reduce your taxable income and potentially lower your tax liability.

7. Plan ahead for taxes: Finally, it is important to plan ahead for taxes throughout the year. This includes keeping track of your income and expenses, setting aside money for taxes, and making estimated tax payments if necessary. By planning ahead, you can avoid surprises come tax time and ensure that you are taking advantage of all available tax-saving strategies.

In conclusion, tax planning and saving strategies are essential for anyone who wants to save money and maximize their income. By understanding tax laws and regulations, taking advantage of tax-deferred retirement accounts, itemizing deductions, making use of tax credits, investing in tax-efficient investments, utilizing employer benefits, and planning ahead for taxes, you can significantly reduce your tax liability and keep more of your hard-earned money.

Understanding Tax Deductions and Credits

Paying taxes is a fact of life for most people, but that doesn't mean you have to pay more than necessary. Tax deductions and credits can help you reduce your tax bill and keep more of your hard-earned money. In this essay, we'll explore the different types of tax deductions and credits, how they work, and how you can take advantage of them.

Tax Deductions

Tax deductions are expenses that can be subtracted from your taxable income, reducing the amount of tax you owe. The most common tax deductions include:

1. Standard deduction: This is a set amount that you can deduct from your taxable income if you don't itemize your deductions. The standard deduction amount varies depending on your filing status, age, and other factors.

Itemized deductions: If your itemized deductions are greater than the standard deduction, you can deduct the higher amount. Itemized deductions include:

State and local taxes

Mortgage interest

Charitable contributions

Medical and dental expenses

Casualty and theft losses

Job expenses and miscellaneous deductions

Above-the-line deductions: These deductions can be taken before you calculate your adjusted gross income (AGI). Above-the-line deductions include:

IRA contributions

Student loan interest

Alimony payments

Health savings account contributions

Tax Credits

Tax credits are even more valuable than tax deductions because they reduce your tax bill on a dollar-for-dollar basis. Some tax credits are refundable, meaning you can receive a refund even if you don't owe any taxes. Here are some of the most common tax credits:

2. Earned Income Tax Credit (EITC): This credit is available to low- and moderate-income taxpayers who work and have earned income. The amount of the credit depends on your income, filing status, and number of children.

3. Child Tax Credit: This credit is worth up to $2,000 per child under age 17. The credit begins to phase out for taxpayers with income above certain levels.

4. American Opportunity Tax Credit: This credit is available to students who are in their first four years of college or other higher education. The

credit is worth up to $2,500 per year and can be used to offset tuition, fees, and course materials.

5. Lifetime Learning Credit: This credit is available to students of all ages who are taking courses to improve their job skills or advance their career. The credit is worth up to $2,000 per year.

6. Child and Dependent Care Credit: This credit is available to taxpayers who pay for child care or care for a disabled dependent while they work. The credit is worth up to 35% of qualifying expenses, depending on your income.

How to Take Advantage of Tax Deductions and Credits

To take advantage of tax deductions and credits, you need to know which ones you qualify for and how to claim them on your tax return. Here are some tips to help you get started:

7. Keep good records: Keep all of your receipts and records of expenses that might be deductible or eligible for a tax credit. This will make it easier to claim the deduction or credit when you file your tax return.

8. Use tax preparation software: Tax preparation software can help you identify deductions and credits that you might be eligible for. The software will ask you questions about your income, expenses, and other factors, and then recommend deductions and credits based on your answers.

9. Consult a tax professional: If you have a complicated tax situation, you may want to consult a tax professional to help you identify all of the deductions and credits you qualify for. A tax professional can also help you navigate any changes to the tax code that might affect your tax situation.

10. Stay informed: Tax laws change, and not knowing them is not an excuse the tax authorities will allow you to use.

Tax-Advantaged Savings Accounts

Tax-advantaged savings accounts are an effective way to save money for various expenses while receiving tax benefits. These accounts come in different forms, each designed for specific purposes. Understanding tax-advantaged savings accounts can help individuals maximize their savings and reduce their tax liabilities.

The most common tax-advantaged savings accounts include 401(k)s, traditional and Roth Individual Retirement Accounts (IRAs), and Health Savings Accounts (HSAs).

401(k)s are offered by employers, allowing employees to contribute a portion of their pre-tax income toward their retirement savings. The contributions are invested and grow tax-deferred until withdrawal during retirement, at which point they are taxed as ordinary income. Additionally, some employers may match a portion of their employees' contributions, further increasing the account's value.

Traditional IRAs allow individuals to contribute a portion of their pre-tax income toward their retirement savings, similar to 401(k)s. However, unlike 401(k)s, individuals can open an IRA independently of their employer. The contributions grow tax-deferred until withdrawal during retirement, at which point they are taxed as ordinary income.

Roth IRAs differ from traditional IRAs in that contributions are made with after-tax income, and the account grows tax-free. Withdrawals during retirement are also tax-free, making Roth IRAs an attractive option for those who anticipate being in a higher tax bracket during retirement.

Health Savings Accounts are designed for those with high-deductible health plans. Contributions to an HSA are tax-deductible, and the account grows tax-free. Withdrawals made for qualified medical expenses are tax-free as well, making HSAs a valuable tool for saving money on healthcare costs.

Another tax-advantaged savings account is the 529 plan, designed specifically for saving money for college expenses. Contributions to a 529 plan are not tax-deductible, but the account grows tax-free, and withdrawals for qualified education expenses are also tax-free.

Utilizing tax-advantaged savings accounts can result in significant tax savings and help individuals reach their savings goals faster. For example, contributing to a 401(k) or traditional IRA can reduce an individual's taxable income, resulting in lower tax liability. Additionally, the tax-deferred growth of these accounts can lead to substantial savings over time.

However, it is important to note that some tax-advantaged savings accounts come with contribution limits and restrictions. For instance, 401(k)s have a maximum annual contribution limit, and there may be penalties for early withdrawals from retirement accounts.

Individuals should also consider their unique financial situation and future goals when choosing which tax-advantaged savings account to utilize. For example, those who anticipate higher healthcare expenses may benefit from an HSA, while those saving for college expenses may prefer a 529 plan.

In conclusion, understanding tax-advantaged savings accounts is crucial for maximizing savings and reducing tax liabilities. Each account comes with its own benefits and restrictions, and individuals should carefully consider their financial situation and future goals when choosing which accounts to utilize. By taking advantage of these accounts, individuals can build wealth and achieve their financial goals more efficiently.

Strategies for Reducing Your Tax Bill

Strategies for Reducing Your Tax Bill

Paying taxes is a necessary obligation that every citizen of a country has to fulfill. Taxes contribute to the development of a country, infrastructure, public services, and other essential areas. However, it is also essential to ensure that you are not overpaying your taxes and taking advantage of all the deductions and credits available to you. In this essay, we will discuss strategies for reducing your tax bill and keeping more money in your pocket.

Take Advantage of Tax Deductions:

One of the most effective ways to reduce your tax bill is to take advantage of tax deductions. Tax deductions lower your taxable income, which in turn reduces the amount of tax you owe. There are various types of tax deductions available, such as deductions for charitable donations, mortgage interest, property taxes, and more. To claim a tax deduction, you must itemize your deductions instead of taking the standard deduction. It's essential to keep track of all your expenses throughout the year and to consult a tax professional to ensure that you are taking advantage of all the deductions available to you.

Contribute to Tax-Advantaged Accounts:

Contributing to tax-advantaged accounts is another effective way to reduce your tax bill. Tax-advantaged accounts include 401(k)s, IRAs, and Health Savings Accounts (HSAs). These accounts allow you to contribute pre-tax dollars, which lowers your taxable income. In addition, earnings within these accounts grow tax-free until you withdraw the funds in retirement. It's essential to contribute as much as possible to these accounts to take advantage of the tax benefits they offer.

Consider Tax Credits:

Tax credits are another way to reduce your tax bill. Tax credits are even more beneficial than tax deductions because they reduce your tax bill dollar-for-dollar. There are various types of tax credits available, such as the Earned Income Tax Credit, Child Tax Credit, and American Opportunity Tax Credit. To claim these tax credits, you must meet certain requirements. For example, to claim the Child Tax Credit, you must have a dependent child under the age of 17. It's essential to research the tax credits available to you and consult a tax professional to ensure that you are taking advantage of all the credits you are eligible for.

Maximize Your Business Deductions:

If you are a business owner, there are various deductions available to you that can reduce your tax bill. Business deductions include expenses such as office rent, employee salaries, and travel expenses. It's essential to keep track of all your business expenses throughout the year and consult a tax professional to ensure that you are taking advantage of all the deductions available to you.

Time Your Capital Gains and Losses:

Capital gains and losses can have a significant impact on your tax bill. If you sell an asset for more than you paid for it, you have a capital gain. If you sell an asset for less than you paid for it, you have a capital loss. Capital gains are subject to taxes, but capital losses can be used to offset capital gains. It's essential to time your capital gains and losses to ensure that you are minimizing your tax bill. For example, if you have a capital gain, you may want to sell an asset that has a capital loss to offset the gain.

In conclusion, paying taxes is an essential obligation that every citizen has to fulfill. However, it's also essential to ensure that you are not overpaying your taxes and taking advantage of all the deductions and credits available to you. By following the strategies outlined in this essay, you can reduce your tax bill and keep more money in your pocket. Remember to consult a tax professional to ensure that you are taking advantage of all the tax benefits available to you.

Chapter Thirteen

Savings Challenges and Strategies

Savings is an essential aspect of personal finance. It is a crucial part of achieving financial stability and independence. However, saving money can be challenging, especially for those living paycheck to paycheck. It requires a lot of discipline, determination, and motivation. There are various challenges that people face when it comes to saving money, such as lack of income, high expenses, debt, and unexpected emergencies. In this essay, we will discuss some of the common challenges people face when it comes to saving money and strategies to overcome them.

One of the biggest challenges people face when it comes to saving money is a lack of income. It can be challenging to save money when you are barely making enough to cover your basic needs. However, there are various strategies you can employ to save money, regardless of your income level. One of the most effective strategies is to create a budget. A budget helps you keep track of your expenses and identify areas where you can cut back. You can also look for ways to increase your income, such as taking on a side job or selling unwanted items.

Another common challenge when it comes to saving money is high expenses. It can be challenging to save money when your expenses are high, and you are barely making ends meet. However, there are several strategies you can employ to reduce your expenses. One of the most effective strategies is to cut back on non-essential expenses, such as eating out, entertainment, and subscriptions. You can also look for ways to reduce your bills, such as negotiating with service providers or finding more affordable alternatives.

Debt is another significant challenge people face when it comes to saving money. Debt can make it challenging to save money because you have to use your income to pay off your debts. However, there are several strategies you can employ to pay off your debts and start saving money. One of the most effective strategies is to create a debt repayment plan. A debt repayment plan helps you prioritize your debts and pay off the ones with the highest interest rates first. You can also look for ways to reduce your interest rates, such as consolidating your debts into one loan.

Unexpected emergencies are also a common challenge when it comes to saving money. Emergencies, such as medical bills, car repairs, or home repairs, can quickly deplete your savings. However, there are several strategies you can employ to prepare for unexpected emergencies. One of the most effective strategies is to create an emergency fund. An emergency fund is a savings account that you use only for emergencies. You should aim to save at least three to six months' worth of living expenses in your emergency fund.

In addition to the above challenges, people also face various barriers to saving money, such as lack of motivation, procrastination, and lack of knowledge. However, there are several strategies you can employ to overcome these barriers. One of the most effective strategies is to set realistic goals. Setting realistic goals helps you stay motivated and focused on your savings. You can also use technology, such as budgeting apps and automatic savings plans, to help you stay on track.

In conclusion, saving money is a crucial aspect of personal finance. However, there are various challenges and barriers that people face when it comes to saving money. These challenges include lack of income, high expenses, debt, unexpected emergencies, lack of motivation, procrastination, and lack of knowledge. To overcome these challenges, you need to employ various strategies, such as creating a budget, cutting back on expenses, creating a debt repayment plan, creating an emergency fund, setting realistic goals, and using technology. By employing these strategies, you can overcome the challenges of saving money and achieve financial stability and independence.

Setting Short-Term and Long-Term Savings Goals

Saving money is an essential part of financial planning. Whether you are saving for an emergency fund, a down payment on a house, or your child's education, setting savings goals is crucial to achieve your financial objectives. Setting realistic and achievable savings goals is a necessary step to stay motivated and on track. In this essay, we will discuss the importance of setting short-term and long-term savings goals, along with some strategies to achieve them.

Short-Term Savings Goals:

Short-term savings goals are typically for expenses that you will need to pay for in the next few months to a year. These goals may include things like paying off credit card debt, saving for a vacation, or an upcoming event such as a wedding or a home renovation project. Having short-term savings goals can help you stay focused and motivated, knowing that you have a specific goal in mind.

One of the best ways to start setting short-term savings goals is to create a budget. A budget helps you keep track of your income and expenses and provides a clear picture of how much money you can save each month. Once you have established your budget, you can set a specific amount of money to save each month towards your short-term goals. For example, if you are planning a vacation, you can estimate how much you will need to save each month to reach your goal and adjust your spending accordingly.

Another strategy to achieve short-term savings goals is to automate your savings. You can set up automatic transfers from your checking account to your savings account each month. This way, you won't forget to save, and the money will be deducted automatically, making it easier to achieve your savings goals.

Long-Term Savings Goals:

Long-term savings goals typically take longer to achieve and require a more extended commitment. These goals may include saving for retirement, your child's education, or a down payment on a house. Saving for long-term goals requires a different strategy than saving for short-term goals. Here are some strategies to achieve your long-term savings goals:

Start Early:

The earlier you start saving for your long-term goals, the easier it will be to reach them. Starting early means you have more time to benefit from compound interest and increase your overall savings.

Invest in Retirement Accounts:

Retirement accounts such as 401(k)s and IRAs are excellent options for saving for retirement. These accounts offer tax advantages and allow your money to grow tax-free. If your employer offers a 401(k) match, be sure to take advantage of it, as this is essentially free money towards your retirement savings.

Save for Education:

If you have children, saving for their education is an essential long-term goal. One option is to open a 529 savings plan, which offers tax-free growth and withdrawals for qualifying education expenses.

Invest in Real Estate:

Investing in real estate can be a long-term savings goal, as it allows you to build equity over time. Owning rental property or investing in real estate investment trusts (REITs) can be a smart long-term investment strategy.

Setting short-term and long-term savings goals is an essential part of financial planning. Short-term savings goals help you stay focused and motivated while achieving your immediate financial objectives, while long-term savings goals require a different strategy and commitment to achieve your future financial objectives. By following the strategies mentioned in this essay, you can create a roadmap for your financial success and achieve your savings goals. Remember, the key is to be disciplined, stay committed to your goals, and adjust your strategy as needed.

Participating in Savings Challenges

Participating in savings challenges can be a great way to jump-start your savings goals and develop healthy financial habits. Savings challenges can take many forms, from short-term challenges focused on cutting back on expenses to long-term challenges aimed at building a substantial emergency fund or saving for a down payment on a home. In this essay, we will explore some common savings challenges and strategies for participating in them effectively.

Short-Term Savings Challenges

Short-term savings challenges typically last for a week or a month and focus on cutting back on a specific expense. One popular example is the "no-spend" challenge, where participants commit to not spending any money on non-essential items for a set period of time. This challenge can be a great way to become more mindful of your spending habits and identify areas where you can cut back.

Another short-term savings challenge is the "pantry challenge," where participants commit to eating only from their pantry and freezer for a set period of time, such as a week or a month. This challenge can help you use up items that have been sitting in your pantry or freezer for a while, saving you money on groceries in the process.

To participate in a short-term savings challenge effectively, it's important to set clear goals and guidelines for yourself. Decide on the length of the challenge and the specific expense you want to focus on cutting back. Make a plan for how you will track your progress and hold yourself accountable. And don't forget to celebrate your successes along the way, no matter how small they may be.

Long-Term Savings Challenges

Long-term savings challenges typically last for several months or even years and focus on building up a substantial savings cushion. One popular example is the "52-week challenge," where participants aim to save a certain amount of money each week for a year. The amount saved increases each week, starting with $1 in week one and increasing by $1 each week until reaching $52 in week 52. By the end of the year, participants will have saved over $1,300.

Another long-term savings challenge is the "emergency fund challenge," where participants aim to save three to six months' worth of living expenses in an emergency fund. This can be a daunting task, but breaking it down into smaller, more manageable goals can make it feel more achievable. For example, you could aim to save one month's worth of expenses in the first three months, two months' worth in the next three months, and so on.

To participate in a long-term savings challenge effectively, it's important to set realistic goals and break them down into smaller, more achievable milestones. Make a plan for how you will track your progress and adjust your goals if necessary. And don't forget to celebrate your successes along the way, no matter how small they may be.

Strategies for Participating in Savings Challenges

Whether you are participating in a short-term or long-term savings challenge, there are several strategies that can help you stay on track and achieve your goals.

First, automate your savings as much as possible. Set up automatic transfers from your checking account to your savings account each month to ensure that you are saving consistently. This can also help you avoid the temptation to spend the money before you have a chance to save it.

Second, get creative with your savings strategies. Look for ways to cut back on expenses that you may not have considered before, such as canceling subscriptions you don't use or switching to a cheaper cell phone plan. Consider ways to earn extra income, such as selling items you no longer need or picking up a side hustle.

Third, find support and accountability. Join a savings challenge group on social media or enlist a friend or family member to participate in the challenge with you. Having someone to share your successes and challenges with can help keep you motivated and accountable.

Creating a Savings Support System

Creating a Savings Support System

Saving money can be a challenging task, especially when you don't have a support system to encourage and motivate you. However, building a savings support system can help you stay on track and achieve your financial goals. In this essay, we will discuss the importance of creating a savings support system and the different ways to build one.

Why Create a Savings Support System?

A savings support system is a group of people or resources that help you save money and achieve your financial goals. It can provide you with the motivation, accountability, and knowledge you need to stick to your savings plan. Here are some reasons why creating a savings support system is important:

1. Motivation and Accountability: When you have a support system, you are more likely to stay motivated and accountable. Your support system can provide you with the encouragement you need to continue saving, even when you feel discouraged.

2. Shared Knowledge: A support system can also provide you with valuable knowledge and resources. For instance, you can learn from others how they have saved money or how to invest in a particular financial product.

3. Collaboration: Collaborating with others can also help you save more money. You can share expenses with others or split the cost of a big-ticket item, such as a car or a home.

Ways to Build a Savings Support System

Here are some ways to build a savings support system:

4. Join a Savings Group: A savings group is a group of individuals who pool their money together to save and invest. Members of the group con-

tribute a set amount of money each month, and the group uses the funds to make investments or provide loans to members. Savings groups can be found online or in your local community.

5. Enlist a Financial Advisor: A financial advisor can provide you with valuable advice and guidance on saving and investing. They can help you create a savings plan and provide you with strategies for achieving your financial goals.

6. Create a Savings Challenge: You can create a savings challenge with friends or family members to motivate each other to save money. For example, you can challenge each other to save a certain amount of money each week or month and reward the person who saves the most.

7. Find an Accountability Partner: An accountability partner is someone who can hold you accountable for your savings goals. This can be a friend or family member who checks in with you regularly to see how you are progressing.

8. Attend Financial Workshops or Seminars: Attending financial workshops or seminars can provide you with valuable knowledge and resources. You can learn about different saving and investing strategies, as well as how to manage your finances effectively.

9. Use Online Resources: There are many online resources available that can help you save money and achieve your financial goals. For example, there are websites that offer tips on saving money, as well as budgeting apps that can help you track your expenses and create a savings plan.

Creating a savings support system is an essential part of achieving your financial goals. Whether you join a savings group, enlist the help of a financial advisor, or challenge yourself with friends and family, having a support system can provide you with the motivation, accountability, and knowledge you need to succeed. So, take the time to build a savings support system today, and start working towards your financial goals.

Chapter Fourteen

Frugal Living Tips and Tricks

Frugal living is all about being resourceful, mindful, and creative in managing your finances. It's about finding ways to live well within your means without sacrificing your quality of life. Here are some frugal living tips and tricks to help you save money and achieve financial freedom.

Create a budget and stick to it.

A budget is a key tool in managing your finances. It helps you track your income and expenses, identify areas where you can cut back, and prioritize your spending. Start by making a list of your monthly expenses, including rent or mortgage, utilities, food, transportation, and entertainment. Then, compare your expenses to your income and see where you can make adjustments. Remember to factor in unexpected expenses, such as car repairs or medical bills, and allocate a portion of your budget towards savings.

Shop smart.

One of the biggest expenses for most people is food. To save money on groceries, plan your meals ahead of time, make a list before you go to the store, and stick to it. Look for coupons and sales, and consider buying generic or store-brand items instead of name brands. When shopping for clothes or household items, try to buy them secondhand at thrift stores, yard sales, or online marketplaces. You can also negotiate prices or ask for discounts on big-ticket items like furniture or appliances.

Cut back on unnecessary expenses.

Take a close look at your monthly bills and see if there are any services you're paying for but not using. Cancel subscriptions or memberships you don't need, and look for ways to reduce your utility bills, such as turning off lights and unplugging electronics when you're not using them. Consider downgrading your phone or internet plan, or bundling services to save money. Also, avoid impulse purchases and think carefully before making a big-ticket purchase.

Find ways to earn extra income.

If you're struggling to make ends meet or want to save more money, consider finding ways to earn extra income. You can take on a part-time job, sell items you no longer need, or offer your services as a freelancer or consultant. You can also participate in online surveys, rent out a spare room on Airbnb, or start a small business on the side.

Practice energy conservation.

Energy costs can add up quickly, so it's important to be mindful of your energy usage. Make sure your home is properly insulated, and switch to energy-efficient light bulbs and appliances. Use a programmable thermostat to regulate your heating and cooling, and turn off lights and appliances when you're not using them. Consider using public transportation or carpooling to save money on gas and parking.

Embrace a minimalist lifestyle.

Minimalism is a lifestyle that focuses on living with less, which can help you save money and reduce your environmental impact. You can start by decluttering your home and getting rid of items you don't need or use. You can also practice mindful consumption by buying only what you need and avoiding impulse purchases. Consider embracing a simpler lifestyle by reducing your dependence on technology, spending more time outdoors, and focusing on relationships and experiences rather than material possessions.

Invest in quality over quantity.

While it may be tempting to buy cheap or disposable items, investing in quality products can save you money in the long run. High-quality items last longer, require less maintenance, and are often more energy-efficient. Consider investing in a good pair of shoes, a durable coat, or a well-made appliance that will last for years.

Prioritize experiences over things.

Instead of spending money on material possessions, prioritize experiences that bring you joy and fulfillment. Travel, volunteer, or pursue hobbies that enrich your life and connect you with others. You can also spend quality time with family and friends, host potlucks or game nights.

Embracing a Minimalist Lifestyle

In recent years, the concept of minimalism has gained popularity as a way of life that emphasizes the value of owning less and living more intentionally. Minimalism can help individuals reduce their expenses, eliminate clutter, and focus on what truly matters in life. In this essay, we will explore the benefits of embracing a minimalist lifestyle and how it can help individuals save money.

Firstly, minimalism encourages people to focus on what is truly important and essential in life. By eliminating unnecessary possessions, individuals can reduce their expenses and save money. For instance, many people spend a significant amount of money on buying clothes, accessories, and gadgets that they do not need. Adopting a minimalist lifestyle can help individuals become more mindful of their consumption habits and spend money on things that add real value to their lives.

In addition, minimalism can help individuals save money by reducing their housing costs. Many people choose to live in large and spacious homes that they do not need, which can be expensive to maintain. By downsizing and living in a smaller home, individuals can reduce their expenses and save money on rent or mortgage payments, utility bills, and other maintenance costs. Furthermore, living in a smaller home can also encourage people to adopt a more minimalist lifestyle, as they have limited space to store their possessions.

Another benefit of minimalism is that it can help individuals save money by reducing their transportation costs. Many people own multiple cars or choose to live in locations that require them to drive long distances to work or run errands. Adopting a minimalist lifestyle can encourage individuals to live in more walkable and bike-friendly neighborhoods or to rely on public transportation. This can help individuals save money on gas, car maintenance, and insurance costs, while also promoting a more sustainable and environmentally friendly way of life.

Furthermore, minimalism can help individuals save money by encouraging them to adopt a more mindful approach to their consumption habits. By choosing to buy only what they need, individuals can reduce their expenses and avoid impulse purchases that often lead to clutter and waste. For instance, instead of buying a new outfit every week, individuals can choose to invest in high-quality and versatile pieces that can be worn for years to come. By adopting a more mindful approach to their consumption habits, individuals can also reduce their environmental footprint and promote a more sustainable way of life.

Finally, minimalism can also help individuals save money by encouraging them to live a more frugal and simple lifestyle. This can involve making conscious choices about how to spend money and finding ways to live more creatively and resourcefully. For instance, instead of eating out at expensive restaurants, individuals can choose to cook meals at home using affordable and nutritious ingredients. Similarly, instead of buying expensive gym memberships, individuals can choose to exercise outdoors or at home using free resources such as YouTube videos or fitness apps. By embracing a more frugal and simple lifestyle, individuals can learn to appreciate the value of what they have and save money for the things that truly matter to them.

In conclusion, adopting a minimalist lifestyle can help individuals reduce their expenses and save money in various ways. By focusing on what is truly important and essential in life, individuals can become more mindful of their consumption habits and spend money on things that add real value to their lives. Whether it involves downsizing their home, relying on public transportation, or adopting a more frugal and simple lifestyle, minimalism can help individuals live more intentionally and save money in the process.

Reducing Waste and Embracing Sustainability

Reducing Waste and Embracing Sustainability

In today's world, sustainability has become a buzzword, and rightly so. We have become more aware of the impact we have on the planet and are now seeking ways to reduce our carbon footprint. One of the ways we can do this is by reducing waste. Not only is reducing waste good for the environment, but it can also save us money. In this essay, we will explore ways we can reduce waste and embrace sustainability while also saving money.

One of the biggest contributors to waste is plastic. Single-use plastic items like water bottles, straws, and plastic bags are everywhere, and they are harmful to the environment. One way to reduce waste is by carrying a reusable water bottle and saying no to single-use plastic bottles. It's estimated that Americans use 50 billion plastic water bottles each year, and only 23% of those are recycled. By carrying a reusable water bottle, we can significantly reduce the amount of plastic we use and also save money. The cost of bottled water is significantly higher than tap water, so by carrying a reusable water bottle, we can save money and reduce waste at the same time.

Another way to reduce waste is by bringing reusable bags to the grocery store. Plastic bags are not only harmful to the environment, but they can also end up costing us money. Many cities and states are now imposing a fee on single-use plastic bags, which can add up over time. By bringing reusable bags to the grocery store, we can save money and reduce waste.

Food waste is another significant contributor to waste. It's estimated that 30-40% of the food supply in the United States is wasted each year. This waste has a significant impact on the environment and also on our wallets. By reducing food waste, we can save money and reduce our carbon footprint. One way to reduce food waste is by meal planning. By planning out our meals for the week and only buying what we need, we can reduce the amount of food that goes to waste. Another way to reduce food waste is by composting. Composting not only reduces waste but also creates nutrient-rich soil that can be used to grow plants, saving us money on fertilizers.

Energy consumption is another significant contributor to waste. By reducing our energy consumption, we can save money and reduce our carbon footprint. One way to reduce energy consumption is by switching to energy-efficient light bulbs. Energy-efficient light bulbs use up to 80% less energy than traditional light bulbs and last up to 25 times longer. This can save us money on our energy bills and also reduce our carbon footprint. Another way to reduce energy consumption is by unplugging electronics when they are not in use. Even when turned off, electronics can still use energy. By unplugging them when not in use, we can save money on our energy bills and also reduce our carbon footprint.

Reducing waste and embracing sustainability is not just good for the environment, it's also good for our wallets. By reducing our use of single-use plastic items, bringing reusable bags to the grocery store, reducing food waste, and reducing energy consumption, we can save money while also reducing our carbon footprint. We can also embrace sustainability by choosing to buy products made from sustainable materials and supporting companies that prioritize sustainability.

In conclusion, reducing waste and embracing sustainability is essential for our planet's health and our wallets. We can all take small steps to reduce our waste and become more sustainable. By carrying a reusable water bottle, bringing reusable bags to the grocery store, reducing food waste, reducing energy consumption, and supporting companies that prioritize sustainability, we can make a positive impact on the environment and save money at the same time.

DIY Projects to Save Money

DIY or do-it-yourself projects have become increasingly popular in recent years. Not only are they a fun and creative way to spend your time, but they can also save you money. Whether it's fixing something in your home, creating your own decor, or even making your own beauty products, DIY projects are a great way to save money and learn new skills. In this essay, we'll discuss some DIY projects you can do to save money.

Fixing and maintaining your home appliances

If your home appliances are not working as well as they used to, don't rush out to buy a new one just yet. Many appliance problems can be easily fixed with some basic tools and know-how. For example, if your refrigerator is not cooling properly, the problem could be a dirty condenser coil. Simply vacuuming or brushing the coil can often solve the problem. Similarly, if your dishwasher is not draining, it could be due to a clogged drain hose. By taking the time to learn how to maintain and repair your appliances, you can save money on costly repairs or replacements.

Creating your own home decor

Home decor can be expensive, but with a little creativity and DIY skills, you can make your own unique pieces for a fraction of the cost. For example, you can create your own wall art using canvas, paint, and stencils. You can also make your own throw pillows by repurposing old fabric or clothes. By creating your own home decor, you can personalize your space and save money.

Making your own cleaning products

Cleaning products can be expensive, and many contain harsh chemicals that can be harmful to your health and the environment. By making your own cleaning products, you can save money and avoid these harmful chemicals. For example, you can make an all-purpose cleaner by mixing vinegar, water, and essential oils. You can also make your own laundry detergent by combining washing soda, Borax, and grated soap. Not only are these DIY cleaning products effective, but they are also eco-friendly.

Repurposing old items

Instead of throwing out old items, try repurposing them into something new. For example, an old dresser can be repurposed into a TV stand, or an old ladder can be turned into a bookshelf. By repurposing old items, you can save money on new furniture or decor, and also reduce waste.

Making your own beauty products

Beauty products can be expensive, but with a few simple ingredients, you can make your own. For example, you can make your own face masks using ingredients like honey, oatmeal, and avocado. You can also make your own body scrub by mixing sugar and coconut oil. By making your own beauty products, you can save money and avoid harsh chemicals found in many store-bought products.

Growing your own food

Growing your own food can be a fun and rewarding experience, as well as a way to save money on groceries. You can start small with a few herbs in a windowsill, or you can create a full vegetable garden in your backyard. By growing your own food, you can ensure that it is fresh and free of harmful pesticides and chemicals.

In conclusion, DIY projects are a great way to save money and learn new skills. Whether it's fixing something in your home, creating your own decor, or making your own beauty products, there are endless possibilities for DIY projects. By embracing a DIY lifestyle, you can save money and reduce waste, while also creating unique and personalized items for your home and life.

Quick list of ways to save money:

Chapter Fifteen

Saving Money on Childcare and Parenting

- Create a budget and stick to it.
- Shop for groceries with a list and stick to it.
- Meal plan and prep at home instead of eating out.
- Reduce energy consumption by turning off lights and unplugging appliances when not in use.
- Use public transportation or carpool instead of driving alone.
- Shop at thrift stores or consignment shops for clothing and household items.
- Use coupons and take advantage of sales.
- DIY home repairs and maintenance instead of hiring a professional.
- Shop for generic or store-brand items.
- Use cash instead of credit cards.
- Cancel unnecessary subscriptions or memberships.
- Negotiate bills, such as cable or phone bills.

- Use a programmable thermostat to save on heating and cooling costs.
- Use a clothesline or drying rack instead of a dryer.
- Cut back on unnecessary expenses, such as eating out or buying coffee.
- Buy in bulk for items you use frequently.
- Use reusable items, such as cloth napkins and shopping bags.
- Repair or repurpose items instead of buying new ones.
- Use a library instead of buying books or movies.
- Reduce water usage by taking shorter showers and fixing leaks.
- Shop for furniture and home decor second-hand.
- Use a refillable water bottle instead of buying bottled water.
- Buy produce in season and freeze or preserve it for later.
- Use a bike or walk instead of driving short distances.
- Cook at home instead of ordering takeout.
- Use a slow cooker to save time and energy.
- Use a cheaper cell phone plan or switch to a prepaid plan.
- Shop for deals on vacations and travel.
- Reduce meat consumption and opt for plant-based meals.

- Use a credit card with rewards or cash back.
- Host potluck dinners instead of going out to eat.
- Use a budgeting app or tool to track expenses.
- Use a community garden or start your own garden.
- Plan ahead for large expenses, such as holidays or home repairs.
- Take advantage of free community events and activities.
- Use a free or low-cost gym instead of paying for a membership.
- Use a free tax filing service or software.
- Rent or borrow items instead of buying them.
- Use a smart power strip to reduce energy usage.
- Use a free budgeting tool to create and track a budget.
- Use a credit card with no annual fee.
- Use a free financial planning tool to track investments and savings.
- Use a prepaid debit card to avoid overdraft fees.
- Use a credit card with a 0% introductory APR for balance transfers.
- Use a prepaid cell phone plan instead of a contract plan.
- Pay bills online to save on postage and paper costs.
- Use a free budgeting tool to track expenses and income.

- Use a free personal finance app to manage finances.
- Use a free investment app to manage investments.
- Use a free financial planning tool to create a long-term financial plan.

Saving Money on Childcare and Parenting

Being a parent can be one of the most rewarding experiences in life, but it can also be incredibly expensive. Between the cost of diapers, baby gear, and childcare, it can be difficult to balance the needs of your family with your financial goals. Fortunately, there are a variety of ways to save money on childcare and parenting expenses without sacrificing the quality of care for your children. In this essay, we'll explore some of the best strategies for saving money on childcare and parenting.

Consider alternative childcare options

One of the biggest expenses for parents is childcare. The cost of daycare, nanny services, or a babysitter can quickly add up, particularly if you need full-time care. However, there are a number of alternative childcare options that can save you money. For example, you could consider enrolling your child in a co-op daycare, where parents take turns providing care. Alternatively, you could look into sharing a nanny with another family to split the cost. Finally, you could consider enrolling your child in a part-time preschool program, which can be less expensive than full-time daycare.

Buy secondhand baby gear

Another major expense for parents is buying baby gear. From strollers to cribs to high chairs, there are a lot of items you'll need to purchase to care for your child. However, buying secondhand baby gear can be a great way to save money. Check out local consignment shops, garage sales, or online marketplaces like Facebook Marketplace or Craigslist to find gently used baby gear at a fraction of the cost of buying new. Just make sure to carefully inspect any items before purchasing to ensure they're in good condition.

Breastfeed

If you're able to breastfeed your child, it can be a great way to save money on formula. Formula can be incredibly expensive, and the cost can add up quickly over time. While breastfeeding may not be an option for everyone, it can be a great way to save money and provide your child with optimal nutrition.

Make your own baby food

Another way to save money on baby-related expenses is to make your own baby food. While pre-made baby food can be convenient, it can also be expensive. By making your own baby food, you can save money and ensure that your child is getting the freshest, healthiest ingredients. You can easily puree fruits and vegetables in a food processor or blender, and freeze portions for later use.

Use cloth diapers

Disposable diapers can be a major expense for parents, particularly if you need to purchase them on a regular basis. However, using cloth diapers can be a great way to save money over time. While the upfront cost of cloth diapers may be higher than buying disposable diapers, they can be reused multiple times, which can save you money in the long run. Additionally, cloth diapers can be better for the environment, as they don't contribute to the waste stream like disposable diapers do.

Take advantage of tax credits

Finally, it's important to remember that there are a number of tax credits available to parents that can help offset the cost of childcare and other parenting expenses. For example, the Child and Dependent Care Tax Credit can help you save money on eligible expenses related to childcare. Additionally, the Earned Income Tax Credit can provide a tax refund for eligible families with low to moderate incomes. Be sure to talk to a tax professional to determine which tax credits you may be eligible for.

Budget-Friendly Childcare Options

Budget-Friendly Childcare Options

For parents, finding affordable and reliable childcare can be a significant challenge. Childcare expenses can quickly become a significant portion of a family's budget, often making it difficult to make ends meet. Fortunately, there are several budget-friendly childcare options available that can help parents save money while still providing quality care for their children.

Family Members or Friends

One of the most obvious budget-friendly childcare options is to ask a family member or friend to care for your child while you work. While this may not always be a feasible option, it can be an excellent way to save money on childcare costs.

If you do decide to go this route, be sure to set clear expectations and boundaries with your family member or friend to avoid any misunderstandings or conflicts. Also, be sure to discuss compensation upfront, so there are no surprises down the road.

In-Home Daycare

In-home daycare providers offer childcare services out of their homes, typically caring for a small group of children. These providers are often less expensive than traditional daycare centers, making them an excellent option for budget-conscious parents.

When choosing an in-home daycare provider, be sure to research their qualifications and ask for references. It's also important to visit the provider's home to ensure that it is clean, safe, and meets your standards.

Cooperative Childcare

Cooperative childcare is a type of childcare in which a group of parents takes turns caring for each other's children. Each parent is responsible for watching all of the children in the group for a set amount of time, usually one day per week.

Cooperative childcare can be a great option for parents who have flexible schedules or who work part-time. It can also be an excellent way to save money on childcare costs while building a support network with other parents.

Nanny Sharing

Nanny sharing is a childcare option in which two or more families hire a nanny to care for their children at the same time. This can be an excellent way to reduce the cost of hiring a nanny while still providing individualized care for each child.

When considering nanny sharing, be sure to discuss expectations and boundaries upfront. It's also important to find families with similar parenting styles and schedules to ensure a good fit.

After-School Programs

After-school programs are a great option for parents who need care for their children after school. These programs offer structured activities and supervision for children until their parents can pick them up.

After-school programs can be less expensive than full-time daycare and can provide children with opportunities to socialize and engage in structured activities.

Youth Programs

Youth programs, such as the YMCA, Boys and Girls Club, or local recreation centers, often offer affordable childcare options for school-age children. These programs may offer before and after-school care, as well as summer camps and other activities.

While youth programs may not provide full-time childcare, they can be an excellent option for parents who need occasional care for their children.

Babysitting Co-Ops

Babysitting co-ops are groups of parents who take turns babysitting for each other's children. Members earn points for watching other children and can then use those points to pay for their own childcare needs.

Babysitting co-ops can be an excellent way to save money on occasional childcare needs, such as date nights or doctor's appointments.

In conclusion, finding affordable and reliable childcare can be a challenge for parents, but there are several budget-friendly options available. By exploring these options and finding the one that works best for your family's needs, you can save money while still providing quality care for your children.

Saving Money on Baby Gear and Clothing

Saving Money on Baby Gear and Clothing

Babies are a wonderful addition to any family, but they can also come with a hefty price tag. Between diapers, food, and clothes, the cost of raising a child can quickly add up. One way to save money is to be smart about your purchases of baby gear and clothing. With some simple strategies and tips, you can make sure that you are getting the best value for your money and that your baby has everything they need without breaking the bank.

Buy Used Items

One of the best ways to save money on baby gear and clothing is to buy used items. Many baby items are only used for a short period of time, so they are often in great condition. Consignment shops, thrift stores, and online marketplaces such as Craigslist and Facebook Marketplace are great places to find used baby items at a fraction of the cost of new ones. When buying used items, make sure to inspect them carefully for any damage or wear and tear.

Shop Off-Season

Another way to save money on baby gear and clothing is to shop off-season. Retailers often offer deep discounts on items that are out of season. For example, you can find great deals on winter coats and snowsuits in the summer months. If you plan ahead and purchase items during the off-season, you can save a lot of money.

Buy in Bulk

Buying baby gear and clothing in bulk can also help you save money. For example, if you know that you will need a lot of diapers, consider buying them in bulk. Many retailers offer discounts for bulk purchases, so you can save money in the long run. Just make sure that you have enough storage space for all of the items you are buying.

Stick to the Basics

When it comes to baby gear and clothing, it can be tempting to buy every cute item that you see. However, sticking to the basics can help you save money. You don't need to buy every gadget and gizmo that is marketed to new parents. Stick to the essentials, such as a car seat, stroller, and baby carrier, and you will save a lot of money.

Borrow or Rent

If you have friends or family members who have recently had a baby, consider borrowing or renting items from them. This can be a great way to save money on baby gear and clothing, especially if you only need an item for a short period of time. Just make sure to return the items in the same condition that you received them.

Look for Sales and Coupons

Always be on the lookout for sales and coupons when shopping for baby gear and clothing. Many retailers offer discounts and promotions on a regular basis. You can also sign up for email newsletters or follow retailers on social media to stay up-to-date on their latest deals.

Make Your Own Baby Gear and Clothing

If you are handy with a sewing machine or knitting needles, consider making your own baby gear and clothing. This can be a fun and creative way to save money. There are many patterns and tutorials available online for making baby clothes, blankets, and toys.

Consider Cloth Diapers

Disposable diapers can be a major expense for new parents. Consider using cloth diapers instead. While the initial investment can be more expensive than a pack of disposable diapers, cloth diapers can be reused over and over again. This can save you a lot of money in the long run.

Take Care of Your Baby Gear and Clothing

Finally, taking care of your baby gear and clothing can help you save money. Make sure to follow the care instructions on the label and wash items in a gentle cycle. Hang items to dry instead of using a dryer, as this can help them last longer.

Low-Cost Activities for Kids and Families

As a parent, finding affordable activities for kids and families can be a challenge. However, it doesn't have to be difficult or expensive. There are many low-cost activities that can be fun and engaging for children and parents alike. In this essay, we will explore some of the best low-cost activities for kids and families.

Nature Walks and Hikes

One of the simplest and most cost-effective ways to get outside and enjoy nature is to go for a walk or hike. Most cities and towns have public parks and nature trails that are free to access. Many parks offer guided nature walks or scavenger hunts that can be fun for kids.

Library Programs

The library is a treasure trove of free activities for kids and families. Most libraries offer storytime and craft programs for children, as well as movie nights and author talks. Many libraries also have free access to online resources such as eBooks, audiobooks, and educational databases.

Free Museum Days

Many museums offer free admission on certain days of the week or month. This can be a great opportunity to introduce children to art, history, and science without breaking the bank. Some museums also offer free family programs and workshops.

DIY Arts and Crafts

Arts and crafts are a great way to get creative with kids and can be done on a budget. Many materials can be found at dollar stores or in the recycling bin. There are also many online tutorials and resources available to get inspiration for new projects.

Outdoor Games and Sports

Getting outside and playing games or sports is a fun way to stay active and spend time as a family. Soccer, basketball, and frisbee are just a few examples of games that can be played with little to no cost. Many parks also have playgrounds, swings, and other equipment for kids to enjoy.

Cooking and Baking

Cooking and baking are not only fun but also teach important life skills. There are many simple and low-cost recipes that can be made with kids. From homemade pizzas to cookies, kids can get involved in the process and feel a sense of pride in the finished product.

Volunteer Work

Volunteering is a great way to teach children about empathy and social responsibility while also providing a valuable service to the community. Many organizations offer family-friendly volunteer opportunities, such as cleaning up a park or serving food at a shelter.

Movie Nights at Home

Movie nights can be a fun and inexpensive way to spend time together as a family. Instead of going to the theater, consider renting or streaming a movie at home. Popcorn and snacks can be made at home for a fraction of the cost of movie theater concessions.

Board Games and Puzzles

Board games and puzzles are a classic way to spend time with family and friends. They are also a great way to exercise the brain and learn new skills. Many thrift stores and garage sales have used games and puzzles for sale at a fraction of the cost of new ones.

Planting and Gardening

Planting a garden or caring for indoor plants is a fun way to teach children about responsibility and the environment. Seeds can be purchased for a few dollars, and many plants can be grown indoors or in small spaces. Watching the plants grow and produce fruits or vegetables can be rewarding for both kids and adults.

In conclusion, there are many low-cost activities for kids and families to enjoy together. From nature walks to cooking and baking, there are many ways to have fun and create lasting memories without breaking the bank. By incorporating these activities into your routine, you can provide a fun and engaging environment for your children while also saving money.

Quick list of free activities:

Chapter Sixteen

Saving Money on Weddings and Other Big Events

- Visit a local park or playground.
- Go on a nature walk or hike.
- Have a picnic in the park.
- Organize a scavenger hunt.
- Create a backyard obstacle course.
- Build a fort or a tent.
- Have a movie day at home.
- Host a board game tournament.
- Make homemade pizza or other snacks.
- Have a dance party.
- Create a DIY craft project.
- Host a tea party or a picnic.
- Play dress-up or make-believe.
- Build and fly a kite.

- Learn a new skill, such as knitting or painting.
- Have a book club or reading marathon.
- Play with sidewalk chalk.
- Host a talent show or a karaoke party.
- Create a DIY science experiment.
- Have a family game night.
- Bake cookies or other treats together.
- Play with Play-Doh or other art supplies.
- Have a water balloon fight.
- Host a backyard Olympics.
- Organize a family photo scavenger hunt.
- Have a family trivia night.
- Create a family time capsule.
- Have a bubble blowing competition.
- Make homemade ice cream or popsicles.
- Play with a pet or visit an animal shelter.
- Visit a local museum or art exhibit.
- Attend a free community event or festival.
- Host a family talent show.

- Go on a bike ride or scooter ride.
- Visit a local library and participate in story time or other events.
- Have a pool day or water park day.
- Play a game of tag or hide and seek.
- Have a family game show night.
- Attend a free concert or community movie screening.
- Go on a virtual field trip to a museum or other educational location.
- Create a family garden or plant flowers.
- Host a family cooking competition.
- Visit a local farmer's market.
- Go on a family road trip or day trip.
- Have a family talent show.
- Attend a free fitness or exercise class.
- Play a game of capture the flag or kickball.
- Host a family spelling bee or vocabulary challenge.
- Create a family scrapbook or photo album.
- Have a family talent night where everyone showcases their unique talents.

When it comes to weddings and other big events, it's easy to get carried away with spending. But with a little creativity and planning, it's possible to have a memorable event without breaking the bank. Here are some tips for saving money on weddings and other big events.

1. Set a budget: The first step in saving money on a big event is to set a budget. Determine how much you can realistically afford to spend and make a plan to stick to it. Consider using a budgeting tool or spreadsheet to help keep track of expenses.

2. Prioritize: Once you have a budget, prioritize your spending. Decide what elements of the event are most important to you and allocate more of your budget to those items. For example, if the food is the most important part of the event, allocate more of your budget towards the catering.

3. Consider alternatives to traditional venues: Wedding venues and event spaces can be expensive. Consider alternative venues, such as public parks or community centers, which may be more affordable.

4. DIY decorations: Decorating for a big event can be costly, but making your own decorations can save money. Consider using Pinterest for inspiration and ideas for DIY decorations.

5. Simplify the menu: A plated meal or a buffet can be expensive. Consider a simpler menu, such as heavy appetizers or a dessert bar, to save money on catering.

6. Buy a gently used dress: Wedding dresses can be very expensive, but buying a gently used dress can save you money. Look for pre-owned wedding dresses online or at consignment shops.

7. Ask for help: Don't be afraid to ask friends and family for help with the event. This can include everything from decorating to food preparation to photography.

8. Cut down on the guest list: The more guests you have, the more expensive the event will be. Consider limiting the guest list to close family and friends to save money.

9. Use technology: There are many tools and apps available to help with planning a big event. Consider using a wedding planning app to help keep track of expenses and tasks.

10. Shop around: Don't be afraid to shop around for vendors and services. Get quotes from multiple vendors and compare prices to find the best deal.

In conclusion, planning a big event can be stressful, but it doesn't have to be expensive. With a little creativity and planning, it's possible to have a memorable event while still saving money. By setting a budget, prioritizing spending, and considering alternative options, you can plan a beautiful event without breaking the bank.

Budgeting for a Wedding

Weddings are an important milestone in many people's lives, but they can also be incredibly expensive. Between the venue, the food, the flowers, and the dress, costs can quickly add up, leaving couples feeling overwhelmed and stressed. However, with proper budgeting and planning, it is possible to have a beautiful wedding without breaking the bank.

The first step in budgeting for a wedding is to determine how much you are willing to spend. This number will depend on a variety of factors, such as your income, savings, and other financial goals. Once you have a set budget, it is important to stick to it as closely as possible.

One way to save money on a wedding is to be flexible with the date and time. Weddings that take place on weekdays or during the off-season are often significantly cheaper than those that take place on weekends or during peak season. Additionally, holding the ceremony and reception at the same venue can also save money on transportation costs.

Another way to cut costs is to be mindful of the guest list. The more people you invite, the more money you will spend on food and other expenses. Consider limiting the guest list to close family and friends, or consider having a smaller ceremony and reception with a larger celebration at a later date.

When it comes to decorations and flowers, there are many ways to save money without sacrificing style. Consider using seasonal flowers, which are often less expensive than out-of-season blooms. Additionally, using candles or other simple decorations can create an elegant atmosphere without the need for expensive floral arrangements.

Food and drinks are often the most expensive part of a wedding, but there are ways to save money in this area as well. Consider serving a buffet-style meal instead of a plated dinner, as this can be more cost-effective. Additionally, serving beer and wine instead of a full bar can also help to cut costs.

Finally, it is important to prioritize what is most important to you and your partner. While it can be tempting to splurge on every aspect of the wedding, it is important to determine what truly matters and allocate funds accordingly. For some couples, this may mean spending more on the venue and food, while for others, it may mean investing in a stunning wedding dress.

In conclusion, budgeting for a wedding requires careful planning and consideration. By being flexible with the date and time, limiting the guest list, and prioritizing what is most important, it is possible to have a beautiful wedding without overspending. By staying within your budget and being mindful of costs, you can start your new life together on solid financial footing.

Saving Money on Party Planning and Hosting

Saving Money on Party Planning and Hosting

Parties and events are a great way to celebrate life's special moments and make memories with loved ones. However, hosting parties can be expensive and put a strain on your budget. From decorations and food to entertainment and activities, the costs can quickly add up. In this essay, we will explore some tips and tricks for saving money on party planning and hosting.

Plan Ahead

One of the most important things you can do to save money on party planning is to plan ahead. Set a budget and stick to it. Make a list of everything you will need for the party, including decorations, food, drinks, and activities. Look for deals and discounts on party supplies and decorations in advance. This will give you time to shop around and find the best deals.

Host at Home

Hosting the party at home is one of the easiest ways to save money. Renting a venue or hiring a caterer can be expensive, and hosting at home allows you to control the costs. You can make your own food, decorations, and entertainment, which can save you a lot of money.

Use Digital Invitations

Traditional paper invitations can be expensive, especially if you are hosting a large party. Instead, use digital invitations. There are many websites and apps available that allow you to create and send digital invitations for free.

This not only saves you money on invitations, but it also makes it easier for your guests to RSVP.

DIY Decorations

Instead of buying expensive decorations, consider making your own. There are many DIY decoration ideas available online that are easy and affordable to make. You can use materials you already have at home or purchase inexpensive items at a craft store. This can save you a lot of money and add a personal touch to your party.

Potluck Style

Instead of providing all the food and drinks yourself, consider having a potluck-style party. Ask your guests to bring a dish or drink to share. This not only saves you money, but it also adds variety to the menu and allows your guests to show off their cooking skills.

BYOB

If you are hosting an adult party, consider having a BYOB (bring your own beverage) policy. This can save you a lot of money on alcohol and allows your guests to bring their favorite drinks. Be sure to provide non-alcoholic drinks as well for those who do not drink.

Use a Playlist

Instead of hiring a DJ or band, create your own playlist for the party. There are many music streaming services available that allow you to create your own playlists for free. This saves you money on entertainment and allows you to tailor the music to your guests' tastes.

Simple Activities

Instead of expensive activities like hiring a magician or renting a bounce house, consider simple activities like board games or a movie night. These activities are affordable and can provide hours of entertainment for your guests.

Buy in Bulk

If you are hosting a large party, consider buying in bulk. Buying in bulk can save you money on food, drinks, and decorations. Many wholesale stores offer discounts for bulk purchases.

Clean-Up Yourself

After the party, instead of hiring a cleaning crew, consider cleaning up yourself. This not only saves you money, but it also allows you to keep track of your party supplies and decorations.

In conclusion, hosting a party does not have to break the bank. With some careful planning and creativity, you can save money on party planning and hosting. From DIY decorations to potluck-style parties, there are many ways to save money without sacrificing the fun and memories that come with hosting a party.

Quick tips:

- Set a budget: Set a budget for your wedding and stick to it.
- Prioritize expenses: Prioritize expenses according to what is most important to you as a couple.
- Choose an off-season date: Choose an off-season date to save on venue and vendor costs.
- Use a non-traditional venue: Consider using a non-traditional venue, such as a park or backyard, to save on venue costs.

- Limit the guest list: Limit the guest list to save on catering and venue costs.
- DIY decorations: Create your own decorations to save on decor costs.
- Use seasonal flowers: Use seasonal flowers to save on floral costs.
- Serve a signature cocktail: Serve a signature cocktail instead of a full bar to save on alcohol costs.
- Limit the menu: Limit the menu to save on catering costs.
- Serve a buffet-style meal: Serve a buffet-style meal instead of a plated meal to save on catering costs.
- Use a friend or family member as a DJ: Use a friend or family member as a DJ instead of hiring a professional.
- Rent instead of buying: Rent items like linens, tables, and chairs instead of buying them.
- Shop sales: Shop for dresses, suits, and accessories during sales to save money.
- Ask for discounts: Ask vendors if they offer discounts for booking multiple services.
- Use digital invitations: Use digital invitations to save on paper and postage costs.
- Skip the save-the-dates: Skip the save-the-dates to save on paper and postage costs.
- Rent bridesmaid dresses: Rent bridesmaid dresses instead of buy-

ing them.

- DIY favors: Create your own wedding favors to save on favor costs.
- Use natural lighting: Schedule your wedding ceremony during the day to save on lighting costs.
- Use a local vendor: Use a local vendor to save on travel and transportation costs.
- Skip the limo: Skip renting a limo and use your own car or a friend's car instead.
- Use a friend or family member as a photographer: Use a friend or family member as a photographer instead of hiring a professional.
- Use a small cake: Use a small wedding cake or cupcakes instead of a large wedding cake to save on dessert costs.
- Skip the wedding planner: Plan your wedding yourself to save on wedding planner costs.
- Use in-season food: Use in-season food to save on catering costs.
- Use natural decor: Use natural decor, such as greenery or branches, to save on decor costs.
- Skip the favors: Skip wedding favors to save on favor costs.
- Serve a dessert bar: Serve a dessert bar instead of a full wedding cake to save on dessert costs.
- Use candles for lighting: Use candles for lighting instead of expensive lighting fixtures.

- Stay local for the honeymoon: Stay local for the honeymoon to save on travel costs.

Reducing Costs for Holiday Celebrations

Holidays are a time for joy and celebration, but they can also be a time of financial stress. Between gift-giving, decorations, and entertaining, the costs can quickly add up. However, there are several ways to reduce the costs of holiday celebrations and make the most out of your budget.

The first step in reducing the costs of holiday celebrations is to set a budget. Determine how much you can realistically afford to spend and stick to that amount. This will help you avoid overspending and prevent unnecessary financial stress.

When it comes to gift-giving, consider setting up a gift exchange or Secret Santa among family and friends. This way, everyone only needs to purchase one gift, reducing the overall costs. You can also consider making homemade gifts, which can be both cost-effective and thoughtful.

For decorations, consider reusing items from previous years or creating your own DIY decorations. Pinterest is a great resource for finding creative and budget-friendly decoration ideas. Additionally, shopping at discount stores or thrift stores can help you find affordable holiday decorations.

When it comes to entertaining, consider hosting a potluck instead of providing all of the food yourself. This way, everyone can contribute a dish, reducing the overall costs. Additionally, consider hosting the party at home instead of going out to a restaurant or event venue, which can be significantly more expensive.

Another way to save money during the holidays is to take advantage of sales and promotions. Black Friday and Cyber Monday are great times to purchase gifts at a discounted price. Additionally, consider purchasing decorations and other holiday items after the holiday has passed, when they are often significantly marked down.

Finally, consider scaling back your holiday celebrations altogether. While it may be difficult to do, reducing the number of gifts or the scale of your decorations and events can significantly reduce the costs. Remember, the true meaning of the holiday season is spending time with loved ones, not the amount of money spent on gifts and festivities.

In addition to these tips, it's important to remember that the most important thing during the holiday season is spending time with loved ones. The memories created during this time are what truly matter, not the amount of money spent on gifts and decorations.

In conclusion, there are several ways to reduce the costs of holiday celebrations and make the most out of your budget. Setting a budget, engaging in gift exchanges, reusing decorations, hosting potlucks, taking advantage of sales and promotions, and scaling back on festivities are all great ways to reduce costs. Remember, the holiday season is about spending time with loved ones, not about overspending on gifts and decorations.

Chapter Seventeen

Saving Money with Technology

Saving money is important, and one of the most effective ways to save money is by utilizing technology. From coupon apps to budgeting software, there are many technological tools available that can help you save money in your everyday life.

One of the most popular ways to save money with technology is through the use of coupon apps. These apps allow you to easily find and use coupons for various products and services, such as groceries, clothing, and entertainment. Popular coupon apps include RetailMeNot, Ibotta, and Coupons.com.

Another way to save money with technology is through budgeting software. Budgeting software helps you track your expenses and create a budget that works for you. Some popular budgeting software options include Mint and You Need a Budget (YNAB). These tools allow you to set financial goals, track your spending, and find areas where you can cut back.

Smart home technology can also help you save money on your utilities. With devices such as smart thermostats and energy-efficient light bulbs, you can easily monitor and control your energy usage. Smart thermostats such as Nest and Ecobee can learn your habits and adjust your heating and cooling accordingly, which can help you save money on your energy bills.

Another way to save money with technology is by utilizing cashback websites and apps. These websites and apps give you cash back on your purchases from participating retailers. Popular options include Rakuten, Swagbucks, and TopCashback.

Online shopping can also be a great way to save money. By shopping online, you can easily compare prices and find the best deals. Many online retailers also offer exclusive discounts and promotions to their online customers. Just be sure to factor in shipping costs when comparing prices.

Finally, if you're looking to save money on entertainment, there are many streaming services available that offer affordable options. Netflix, Hulu, and Amazon Prime Video all offer access to a wide variety of movies and TV shows at a fraction of the cost of cable or satellite TV.

In conclusion, technology can be a powerful tool when it comes to saving money. From coupon apps to budgeting software, there are many options available that can help you cut back on your expenses. By utilizing these tools and being mindful of your spending habits, you can take control of your finances and work towards a more secure financial future.

Utilizing Apps and Tools for Budgeting and Saving

Utilizing Apps and Tools for Budgeting and Saving

In today's digital age, there are countless apps and tools available that can help you manage your finances, budget your money, and save for your financial goals. From personal finance apps to investment tracking tools, these apps can provide valuable insights into your spending habits and help you make informed decisions about your money. Here are some of the best apps and tools for budgeting and saving:

Mint

Mint is one of the most popular personal finance apps on the market. It allows you to connect all of your bank accounts, credit cards, and investment accounts in one place, giving you a comprehensive overview of your finances. With Mint, you can track your spending, set up budgets, and get alerts when you overspend or when bills are due. It also provides personalized insights and recommendations to help you save money.

YNAB

YNAB (You Need A Budget) is another popular budgeting app that helps you track your spending and create a budget. Unlike other budgeting apps, YNAB emphasizes the importance of giving every dollar a job, so you're never caught off guard by unexpected expenses. It also offers financial coaching and personalized support to help you stay on track.

Acorns

Acorns is an investment app that helps you save money by investing your spare change. When you make a purchase with a linked debit or credit card, Acorns rounds up the purchase to the nearest dollar and invests the difference in a portfolio of low-cost ETFs. It also offers a cash-back rewards program and a retirement account option.

Digit

Digit is an app that analyzes your spending habits and automatically saves money for you. It uses algorithms to determine how much money you can afford to save each day and transfers it to a separate savings account. Digit also offers overdraft protection and a 1% savings bonus.

Personal Capital

Personal Capital is a comprehensive financial planning tool that allows you to track your net worth, monitor your investments, and create a personalized financial plan. It also offers retirement planning tools and personalized investment advice.

Honey

Honey is a browser extension that helps you save money while shopping online. It automatically searches for coupon codes and applies them at checkout, saving you money on your purchases. It also offers cash-back rewards and price drop alerts.

Truebill

Truebill is a bill negotiation and management app that helps you lower your monthly bills. It analyzes your bills and subscriptions to identify areas where you can save money and negotiates with providers on your behalf. It also helps you track your spending and cancel subscriptions you no longer need.

Trim

Trim is a financial management tool that helps you save money by automating your finances. It analyzes your spending patterns to identify areas where you can save money, such as by cancelling subscriptions or negotiating bills. It also offers a debt payoff calculator and a savings account option.

Goodbudget

Goodbudget is a budgeting app that uses the envelope method to help you manage your money. It allows you to allocate your money into different virtual envelopes for different expenses, such as groceries, rent, and entertainment. You can track your spending in each envelope to ensure you're staying within your budget.

Robinhood

Robinhood is an investment app that allows you to trade stocks, ETFs, and cryptocurrencies for free. It also offers a cash management account and a premium subscription service with additional features.

Reducing Technology and Subscription Costs

Reducing Technology and Subscription Costs

With the widespread use of technology and the internet, it's easy to get caught up in the latest gadgets and subscription services. However, the cost of these can quickly add up, leaving you with a significant dent in your budget. In this essay, we'll explore some strategies for reducing technology and subscription costs, allowing you to save money and put it towards your other financial goals.

Evaluate Your Technology Needs

The first step in reducing technology costs is to evaluate your needs. Do you really need the latest smartphone or the most expensive laptop? Can you get by with an older model or a refurbished device? Take a look at your usage patterns and determine what features and specifications you really need. You may find that you can save a significant amount of money by opting for a more basic device.

Consider Open Source Alternatives

If you're using paid software programs, consider switching to open-source alternatives. Open-source software is free to use and can provide the same or similar functionality as paid software. For example, instead of paying for Microsoft Office, you can use Google Docs, which is free and has similar features. Similarly, instead of paying for Adobe Photoshop, you can use GIMP, which is a free alternative.

Share Streaming Services with Friends and Family

Streaming services like Netflix, Amazon Prime, and Hulu can be costly if you're paying for them individually. Instead, consider sharing a subscription with friends or family members. Many of these services allow multiple users to use the same account, so you can split the cost and save money.

Bundle Your Services

Another way to save money on subscriptions is to bundle your services. Many companies offer discounted rates if you sign up for multiple services at once. For example, you can bundle your internet, cable, and phone services with one provider and save money on each individual service.

Look for Discounts and Coupons

Before signing up for a subscription service, check for discounts and coupons. Many companies offer introductory rates or discounts for students, military members, and other groups. You can also search for online coupons to save money on your subscription fees.

Cancel Unused Subscriptions

If you have subscriptions that you're not using, cancel them. It's easy to forget about a subscription that's automatically renewed each month or year, but these costs can add up over time. Take a look at your bank and credit card statements to see what subscriptions you're currently paying for, and cancel any that you're not using.

Negotiate with Your Service Providers

Don't be afraid to negotiate with your service providers to get a better rate. If you've been a loyal customer for a long time, you may be able to get a discount or better rate by calling and asking. You can also ask for a discount if you're willing to sign a long-term contract or bundle your services.

DIY Repairs and Upgrades

Instead of paying for repairs or upgrades for your devices, consider doing them yourself. Many online tutorials and videos can guide you through simple repairs or upgrades, such as replacing a cracked screen or adding more memory to your computer. By doing these tasks yourself, you can save a significant amount of money.

Buy Used Devices and Accessories

If you do need to upgrade or replace your devices, consider buying used instead of new. You can find used smartphones, laptops, and other devices for significantly less than the cost of new ones. You can also save money on accessories like chargers, cases, and cables by buying used.

Taking Advantage of Online Resources and Education

Taking Advantage of Online Resources and Education

In today's digital age, online resources and education are becoming increasingly popular as a way to learn new skills, access information, and save money. With the rise of the internet, there are countless opportunities for people to learn and grow without having to leave their homes or spend a lot of money. In this essay, we will explore how taking advantage of online resources and education can help people save money and improve their lives.

One of the biggest advantages of online resources and education is that they are often free or low-cost. There are countless websites, courses, and tutorials available online that can help people learn new skills, improve their knowledge, and even earn certifications or degrees. Many of these resources are provided by reputable institutions and organizations, making them a reliable and effective way to learn.

For example, online courses and tutorials can be an affordable way to learn new skills or improve existing ones. Websites like Coursera, Udemy, and Khan Academy offer a wide range of courses on topics ranging from programming to personal finance to cooking. Many of these courses are free or low-cost, making them accessible to anyone with an internet connection. By taking advantage of these resources, people can develop new skills that can help them in their careers or personal lives.

Another way that online resources and education can save people money is by providing access to information that they might otherwise have to pay for. For example, many online resources offer free or low-cost access to books, articles, and research papers. This can be particularly useful for students or researchers who need to access a large amount of information for their work.

Additionally, online resources and education can be a valuable tool for people who are looking to start a business or launch a new career. There are many websites and resources available that can provide advice and guidance on topics like entrepreneurship, marketing, and business management. By taking advantage of these resources, people can gain valuable knowledge and skills that can help them succeed in their chosen field.

One of the other benefits of online resources and education is that they are often more flexible than traditional educational institutions. Online courses and tutorials can be taken at any time, from anywhere, making them ideal for people who have busy schedules or live in remote areas. This can be particularly useful for people who are working or raising a family, as they can fit their learning around their other commitments.

Finally, online resources and education can be a great way for people to connect with others who share their interests or goals. Many online communities exist that are focused on topics like personal finance, health and wellness, or entrepreneurship. By joining these communities, people can connect with others who share their interests and goals, and share knowledge and advice.

In conclusion, taking advantage of online resources and education can be an excellent way for people to save money and improve their lives. By accessing free or low-cost courses, tutorials, and resources, people can learn new skills, access valuable information, and connect with others who share their interests and goals. With the internet providing endless opportunities for learning and growth, there has never been a better time to take advantage of these resources and start investing in oneself.

Chapter Eighteen

Saving Money on Home Purchases and Renovations

Saving money on home purchases and renovations can be a challenging task, especially for those who are on a tight budget. However, with careful planning and research, it is possible to save a significant amount of money while still achieving your desired home improvements. In this essay, we will explore some strategies and tips for saving money on home purchases and renovations.

Research and Plan

One of the most important steps in saving money on home purchases and renovations is to research and plan carefully. Before making any purchases or beginning any renovations, take the time to research and compare prices, materials, and contractors. This will help you identify areas where you can save money and make informed decisions about your home improvements.

Additionally, creating a detailed plan for your home renovations can help you avoid unnecessary expenses and ensure that you stay within your budget. Be sure to prioritize your needs and wants and consider the long-term costs and benefits of each renovation.

Consider Buying a Fixer-Upper

Buying a fixer-upper can be an excellent way to save money on home purchases. While fixer-uppers may require significant renovations and repairs, they are often priced lower than move-in ready homes. By buying a fixer-upper, you can purchase a home in a desirable location and make renovations over time, allowing you to spread out the costs and save money on the purchase price.

Shop Around for Materials

When purchasing materials for your home renovations, be sure to shop around and compare prices. Consider buying materials in bulk or searching for deals and discounts online or at home improvement stores. Additionally, consider purchasing gently used or recycled materials, which can be significantly cheaper than brand new materials.

DIY Renovations

Another way to save money on home renovations is to do some or all of the work yourself. DIY renovations can be a cost-effective way to make significant improvements to your home. However, it is important to be realistic about your skills and abilities and to consult with professionals when necessary. Additionally, be sure to invest in high-quality tools and materials to ensure that your DIY renovations are safe and effective.

Energy-Efficient Upgrades

Investing in energy-efficient upgrades can be an excellent way to save money on home purchases and renovations over the long-term. Energy-efficient upgrades, such as insulation, solar panels, and energy-efficient appliances, can help reduce your monthly energy bills and save you money over time. Additionally, many energy-efficient upgrades may be eligible for tax credits or rebates, providing even more savings.

Prioritize Repairs Over Renovations

When it comes to home improvements, it is important to prioritize necessary repairs over cosmetic renovations. While cosmetic renovations may be more aesthetically pleasing, necessary repairs, such as fixing leaky roofs or replacing faulty electrical systems, are critical to the safety and longevity of your home. By prioritizing necessary repairs, you can ensure that your home is safe and functional, while still saving money on home improvements.

Consider Alternative Financing Options

If you are unable to pay for your home renovations upfront, consider alternative financing options. Home equity loans, personal loans, and credit cards can provide the necessary funds to make home improvements, but be sure to compare interest rates and fees before selecting a financing option. Additionally, consider working with a financial advisor or professional to help you make informed decisions about financing your home improvements.

In conclusion, saving money on home purchases and renovations requires careful planning, research, and consideration. By prioritizing necessary repairs, shopping around for materials, and considering alternative financing options, you can make significant improvements to your home while still staying within your budget. Additionally, investing in energy-efficient upgrades and considering DIY renovations can provide even more savings over the long-term.

Tips for First-Time Homebuyers

Buying a home can be an exciting and rewarding experience, but it can also be overwhelming and stressful, especially for first-time homebuyers. With so many factors to consider, such as location, price, and financing options, it can be challenging to navigate the process. However, with some careful planning and research, you can make informed decisions that will help you find the right home and save money in the process.

Here are some tips for first-time homebuyers:

Determine your budget

Before you start looking for homes, it's important to determine how much you can afford to spend. Consider your income, expenses, and debts to calculate how much you can comfortably afford to pay each month for your mortgage, insurance, taxes, and other housing expenses. Use online calculators to help you estimate your monthly payments based on different interest rates and down payment amounts.

Get pre-approved for a mortgage

Getting pre-approved for a mortgage can give you a better idea of how much you can afford to spend on a home and can make you a more competitive buyer. Pre-approval also shows sellers that you are a serious buyer who is ready and able to make an offer. Shop around for different lenders to find the best interest rates and terms for your needs.

Choose the right location

The location of your home can have a significant impact on its value and your quality of life. Consider factors such as proximity to work, schools, public transportation, and amenities such as parks, restaurants, and shopping. Research crime rates, property values, and zoning regulations in the areas you are considering to ensure you are making an informed decision.

Hire a real estate agent

A good real estate agent can help you navigate the homebuying process, negotiate the best deal, and find homes that meet your criteria. Look for an agent who has experience in your desired location, has a good reputation, and is willing to communicate with you regularly throughout the process.

Consider the condition of the home

When looking at homes, consider the condition of the property and any potential repairs or renovations that may be needed. A home inspection can help you identify any issues before you make an offer and negotiate repairs or a lower price. Be realistic about your ability to handle DIY projects or the costs of hiring professionals for repairs and renovations.

Don't skip the home inspection

A home inspection is a crucial step in the homebuying process, as it can uncover potential issues with the property that you may not have noticed. It's important to hire a reputable inspector who will thoroughly evaluate the property and provide a detailed report of their findings.

Negotiate the price

Once you have found a home that meets your needs, it's time to make an offer. Work with your real estate agent to determine a fair price based on the condition of the property, market trends, and your budget. Don't be afraid to negotiate with the seller to try to get the best deal possible.

Consider all of the costs

When budgeting for your home purchase, don't forget to consider all of the costs involved. These can include closing costs, property taxes, homeowner's insurance, and maintenance and repairs. Be sure to have a realistic understanding of your total monthly housing expenses to ensure you can afford your home in the long term.

Be patient

Buying a home can be a time-consuming process, and it's important to be patient and not rush into a decision. Take the time to do your research, shop around for the best financing options, and carefully evaluate each home you consider. With some patience and persistence, you can find the right home for you and your budget.

Budgeting for Home Improvements

Budgeting for home improvements can be a challenging task, but it's essential to ensure that your home is comfortable, safe, and efficient. Whether you're planning a major renovation or just want to make some minor upgrades, there are several things you can do to save money and stick to your budget.

The first step in budgeting for home improvements is to determine what needs to be done. Make a list of all the projects you want to complete, and prioritize them based on importance. For example, if your roof is leaking, that should be at the top of the list, while updating your kitchen countertops may be lower on the list.

Once you've identified your projects, you should research the cost of materials and labor. You can do this by getting quotes from contractors or by researching prices online. Keep in mind that some projects may require permits, which can add to the cost.

It's also important to set a budget for each project and stick to it. It's easy to get carried away with home improvements and overspend, but this can lead to financial stress and even debt. To avoid overspending, create a realistic budget for each project and stick to it.

One way to save money on home improvements is to do some of the work yourself. Depending on your skills and experience, you may be able to tackle some projects, such as painting or installing light fixtures, on your own. However, be realistic about your abilities and don't attempt projects that are beyond your skill level.

Another way to save money is to shop around for materials and supplies. Check out online retailers and home improvement stores to compare prices and find the best deals. You may also want to consider buying used or refurbished items, such as appliances or furniture, to save money.

If you're planning a major renovation, it's important to consider the return on investment. While some upgrades, such as a new roof or HVAC system, may not add much to the resale value of your home, other improvements, such as a kitchen remodel or bathroom renovation, can increase the value of your home and provide a good return on investment.

To save money on a major renovation, you may want to consider doing the work in stages. For example, instead of remodeling your entire kitchen at once, you could replace the cabinets and countertops one year and install new appliances the next. This allows you to spread out the cost and avoid taking on too much debt.

It's also important to consider the energy efficiency of your home when planning home improvements. Upgrading to energy-efficient appliances and installing insulation can help you save money on utility bills and reduce your environmental impact. You may also be eligible for tax credits or rebates for energy-efficient upgrades.

Finally, be prepared for unexpected expenses. No matter how carefully you plan, there may be unexpected costs that arise during home renovations. Set aside some extra money in your budget to cover these expenses, so you're not caught off guard.

In conclusion, budgeting for home improvements can be a challenging task, but it's important to ensure that your home is safe, comfortable, and efficient. To save money on home improvements, make a list of projects, research the cost of materials and labor, set a realistic budget, shop around for materials, consider doing some of the work yourself, and be prepared for unexpected expenses. By following these tips, you can improve your home without breaking the bank.

DIY Home Renovations and Upgrades

DIY home renovations and upgrades can be a great way to save money while improving the look and functionality of your home. With the right tools, knowledge, and resources, you can tackle a wide range of projects on your own, without the need to hire expensive contractors.

One of the most significant advantages of DIY home renovations and upgrades is that you have complete control over the project. You can choose the materials, designs, and finishes that best suit your taste and budget. This allows you to create a space that truly reflects your personality and style, without breaking the bank.

Another benefit of DIY home renovations and upgrades is that they can increase the value of your property. By improving the functionality, efficiency, and appearance of your home, you can attract potential buyers and increase your chances of getting a higher price when you decide to sell.

So, how can you get started with DIY home renovations and upgrades? Here are some tips and ideas to help you save money while achieving your dream home:

Plan and research before starting a project

Before starting any DIY home renovation or upgrade, it's essential to do your research and plan accordingly. This includes researching materials, tools, techniques, and safety precautions, as well as creating a budget and timeline for the project. Having a solid plan in place can help you avoid costly mistakes and unexpected expenses down the road.

Start small and build up your skills

If you're new to DIY home renovations and upgrades, it's a good idea to start with smaller projects and build up your skills over time. This can help you gain confidence and experience, as well as prevent you from taking on projects that are beyond your level of expertise.

Invest in quality tools and materials

Investing in quality tools and materials may cost more upfront, but it can save you money in the long run by reducing the need for repairs and replacements. Plus, high-quality materials can improve the durability and longevity of your home renovations and upgrades.

Recycle and repurpose materials

Instead of buying new materials for your DIY home renovations and upgrades, consider recycling and repurposing existing materials. This can include using old furniture, doors, or windows for new projects, or repurposing scraps of wood or metal for decorative accents or functional items.

Get creative with design and decor

DIY home renovations and upgrades also offer an opportunity to get creative with design and decor. Instead of purchasing expensive pre-made decor items, consider creating your own using materials you already have or finding affordable options at thrift stores or online marketplaces.

Take advantage of free resources

There are many free resources available to help you with DIY home renovations and upgrades. These include online tutorials, instructional videos, and community workshops. Taking advantage of these resources can help you learn new skills and techniques, as well as save money on professional services.

In conclusion, DIY home renovations and upgrades can be a fun and cost-effective way to improve the look and functionality of your home. With proper planning, research, and resources, you can tackle a wide range of projects on your own, without the need to hire expensive contractors. So, roll up your sleeves, put on your safety glasses, and get ready to transform your home one project at a time!

Chapter Nineteen

Financial Planning and Goal Setting

Financial planning and goal setting are crucial steps towards achieving financial stability and success. No matter what stage of life you are in, having a solid financial plan in place can help you make the most of your money, achieve your financial goals, and build a more secure financial future for yourself and your family.

The first step in financial planning is setting financial goals. These goals could be short-term or long-term and could include anything from building an emergency fund to saving for retirement. To set effective financial goals, it's important to be specific, realistic, and measurable. For example, instead of setting a vague goal like "save more money," a more specific and measurable goal might be "save $5,000 in an emergency fund by the end of the year."

Once you have set your financial goals, it's time to create a plan to achieve them. This plan should include a detailed budget that outlines your income, expenses, and savings goals. To create an effective budget, you'll need to track your expenses, identify areas where you can cut back, and prioritize your spending to ensure you're putting your money towards the things that matter most to you.

One key component of financial planning is managing debt. If you have debt, it's important to make a plan to pay it off as quickly as possible. This might mean creating a debt repayment plan, consolidating your debt, or seeking out professional help from a financial advisor or credit counselor.

In addition to managing debt, it's important to build and maintain a strong credit score. Your credit score can impact everything from your ability to get a loan or credit card to your insurance rates and even your job prospects. To build a strong credit score, make sure to pay all your bills on time, keep your credit utilization low, and avoid opening too many new lines of credit at once.

Another important aspect of financial planning is building an emergency fund. An emergency fund is a savings account that you can use to cover unexpected expenses like car repairs, medical bills, or job loss. Ideally, you should aim to have three to six months' worth of living expenses saved in your emergency fund. To build your emergency fund, consider automating your savings, putting any unexpected windfalls or bonuses towards your savings, and avoiding unnecessary expenses.

When it comes to investing, it's important to be strategic and informed. Investing can be a powerful tool for building long-term wealth, but it also carries risks. To invest wisely, start by educating yourself about the different types of investments, like stocks, bonds, and mutual funds. Then, consider working with a financial advisor or doing extensive research to develop a long-term investment strategy that aligns with your goals and risk tolerance.

Finally, it's important to regularly review and adjust your financial plan as your goals and circumstances change. Life is unpredictable, and your financial plan should be able to adapt to whatever comes your way. By regularly reviewing your plan and making adjustments as needed, you can stay on track towards achieving your financial goals and building a more secure financial future.

In conclusion, financial planning and goal setting are critical steps towards achieving financial stability and success. By setting specific and measurable financial goals, creating a detailed budget, managing debt, building an emergency fund, investing wisely, and regularly reviewing and adjusting your plan, you can make the most of your money and build a more secure financial future for yourself and your family.

Creating a Financial Roadmap for Your Future

Creating a Financial Roadmap for Your Future

Financial planning is an essential part of building a secure and comfortable future. It involves assessing your current financial situation, setting realistic goals, and creating a plan to achieve those goals. A financial roadmap is a guide that helps you stay on track and make smart financial decisions. In this essay, we will discuss the importance of creating a financial roadmap and how to create one.

Assessing Your Current Financial Situation

The first step in creating a financial roadmap is to assess your current financial situation. This includes calculating your income, expenses, assets, and liabilities. Understanding your current financial situation will help you determine where you stand and what you need to do to achieve your financial goals.

When assessing your current financial situation, it is important to be honest and thorough. Be sure to include all sources of income and all expenses, including fixed expenses like rent or mortgage payments, utilities, and insurance, as well as variable expenses like food, entertainment, and travel.

Setting Realistic Goals

Once you have a clear understanding of your current financial situation, the next step is to set realistic financial goals. Your goals should be specific, measurable, achievable, relevant, and time-bound (SMART). Examples of financial goals might include:

Saving for a down payment on a house

Paying off credit card debt

Saving for retirement

Building an emergency fund

When setting financial goals, it is important to be realistic and specific. For example, if your goal is to save for a down payment on a house, you should determine how much money you need to save and by when. This will help you create a plan to achieve your goal.

Creating a Plan to Achieve Your Goals

Once you have established your financial goals, the next step is to create a plan to achieve them. Your plan should include specific actions you will take to reach your goals. This might include:

Creating a budget to manage your expenses

Finding ways to increase your income

Saving a certain amount of money each month

Investing in a retirement account

Paying off high-interest debt first

Your plan should also take into account any potential obstacles or challenges you may encounter along the way. For example, if you have a high-interest credit card, you may need to focus on paying it off before you can start saving for a down payment on a house.

Tracking Your Progress

Once you have created a plan to achieve your financial goals, it is important to track your progress. This will help you stay motivated and make adjustments as needed. Regularly reviewing your finances and tracking your progress can also help you identify areas where you can make changes to improve your financial situation.

There are several tools and resources available to help you track your progress, including:

Personal finance apps that track your spending and savings

Budgeting software that helps you create and manage a budget

Online calculators that can help you determine how long it will take to reach your financial goals

Revising Your Financial Roadmap

It is important to remember that your financial situation and goals may change over time. It is essential to regularly review and revise your financial roadmap as needed. This may involve adjusting your budget, revising your goals, or finding new ways to increase your income.

Regularly revising your financial roadmap can help you stay on track and make the most of your financial resources. It is important to be flexible and willing to make changes when necessary.

Conclusion

Creating a financial roadmap is an essential part of achieving financial security and comfort. It involves assessing your current financial situation, setting realistic goals, creating a plan to achieve those goals, tracking your progress, and revising your plan as needed. By following these steps, you can take control of your financial future and achieve your long-term financial goals.

Adjusting Your Savings Strategy Over Time

Saving money is an important part of personal finance, but it's not a one-size-fits-all approach. Everyone's financial situation is unique, and therefore, their savings strategy should reflect that. As you go through different stages of life, your financial goals and priorities may change, and it's important to adjust your savings strategy accordingly.

When you're just starting out in your career, your financial focus may be on building an emergency fund and paying off student loans. As you progress in your career and start to earn more income, your focus may shift to saving for a down payment on a house or investing for retirement.

Regardless of where you are in life, it's important to regularly evaluate your savings strategy and make adjustments as necessary. Here are some tips for adjusting your savings strategy over time:

Reevaluate Your Goals

The first step in adjusting your savings strategy is to reevaluate your financial goals. Consider what's most important to you right now, and what you hope to achieve in the future. If your priorities have shifted, your savings strategy should reflect that.

For example, if you've recently gotten married and are planning to start a family, your financial goals may now include saving for a down payment on a larger home or saving for your children's education. On the other hand, if you've recently become an empty nester, your goals may shift to maximizing your retirement savings or saving for travel.

Evaluate Your Budget

Once you've reevaluated your financial goals, it's important to evaluate your budget to ensure that your savings strategy is feasible. Look at your monthly income and expenses, and determine how much you can realistically save each month.

If you're struggling to save as much as you'd like, consider ways to cut back on expenses or increase your income. This could include negotiating a raise at work, freelancing on the side, or finding ways to reduce your monthly bills.

Adjust Your Savings Rate

Based on your updated financial goals and budget, you may need to adjust your savings rate. This means increasing or decreasing the percentage of your income that you're putting toward savings each month.

If your financial goals have become more ambitious, you may need to increase your savings rate to make them achievable. On the other hand, if you're struggling to save as much as you'd like, you may need to decrease your savings rate temporarily until you can get back on track.

Explore New Savings Strategies

As your financial goals and priorities change, you may need to explore new savings strategies to achieve them. This could include opening a new savings account with a higher interest rate, investing in stocks or mutual funds, or exploring alternative investments like real estate or cryptocurrency.

It's important to do your research and consider the risks and potential rewards of any new savings strategy before you commit. You may also want to consult with a financial advisor to get professional guidance on your investment strategy.

Regularly Review and Adjust

Finally, it's important to regularly review and adjust your savings strategy as necessary. This means checking in on your progress toward your financial goals and adjusting your savings rate or strategy as needed.

Set aside time each quarter or year to review your financial situation and adjust your savings strategy accordingly. By regularly reviewing and adjusting your strategy, you can ensure that you're on track to achieve your financial goals.

In conclusion, adjusting your savings strategy over time is an important part of achieving your financial goals. By reevaluating your goals, evaluating your budget, adjusting your savings rate, exploring new savings strategies, and regularly reviewing and adjusting, you can ensure that your savings strategy reflects your unique financial situation and helps you achieve your financial goals.

Building Wealth Through Saving and Investing

Building Wealth Through Saving and Investing

Saving money and investing are two critical aspects of building wealth. By saving money, individuals can accumulate a nest egg, while investing can help grow that nest egg over time. While the process of building wealth through saving and investing can seem daunting, there are several strategies that can help individuals achieve their financial goals.

The Importance of Saving

Saving money is an essential part of building wealth. Saving allows individuals to accumulate funds that can be used to achieve their financial goals. It can also provide a financial cushion in case of an emergency or unexpected expense.

There are several strategies individuals can use to save money. One of the most effective is to establish a budget. A budget helps individuals track their expenses and identify areas where they can reduce spending. By cutting back on unnecessary expenses, individuals can redirect those funds towards saving.

Another effective saving strategy is to automate savings. By setting up automatic contributions to a savings account, individuals can ensure that they are consistently saving money. This can be especially helpful for those who have trouble sticking to a budget or tend to overspend.

The Importance of Investing

Investing is another critical aspect of building wealth. While saving allows individuals to accumulate funds, investing can help those funds grow over time. There are several investment options available, including stocks, bonds, and real estate.

Stocks are one of the most popular investment options. They offer the potential for high returns but also come with a higher level of risk. Bonds, on the other hand, are generally considered to be lower risk but offer lower returns.

Real estate can also be a lucrative investment option. By purchasing rental properties, individuals can generate passive income that can help grow their wealth over time.

The Importance of Diversification

One of the keys to successful investing is diversification. Diversification involves spreading investments across multiple asset classes to reduce risk. By diversifying, individuals can minimize the impact of any single investment on their overall portfolio.

There are several ways to diversify a portfolio. One option is to invest in mutual funds or exchange-traded funds (ETFs). These investment vehicles allow individuals to invest in a diversified portfolio of stocks or bonds. Another option is to invest in a target-date fund. These funds automatically adjust the asset allocation based on the investor's age, gradually shifting to more conservative investments as the individual approaches retirement.

The Importance of Risk Management

While investing can help grow wealth, it also comes with risks. To mitigate these risks, it is essential to have a risk management strategy in place. This strategy should include measures such as diversification, asset allocation, and a long-term investment horizon.

Another critical aspect of risk management is to maintain an emergency fund. An emergency fund is a savings account that can be used to cover unexpected expenses such as job loss or medical bills. By having an emergency fund in place, individuals can avoid having to sell investments during a downturn in the market.

The Importance of Seeking Professional Advice

Building wealth through saving and investing can be complex, and it can be helpful to seek professional advice. Financial advisors can provide guidance on investment options, risk management strategies, and tax-efficient investing. They can also help individuals create a financial plan that takes into account their unique circumstances and goals.

Conclusion

Building wealth through saving and investing is a long-term process that requires patience, discipline, and a solid strategy. By establishing a budget, automating savings, diversifying investments, and managing risk, individuals can achieve their financial goals over time. Seeking professional advice can also be helpful in developing a comprehensive financial plan that takes into account an individual's unique circumstances and goals.

Chapter Twenty

Financial Independence and Early Retirement

Financial independence and early retirement are two concepts that go hand in hand. Achieving financial independence allows you to have the option to retire early if you desire. The concept of financial independence is becoming increasingly popular as more people realize the benefits of being financially free. In this essay, we will explore what financial independence and early retirement mean, the benefits of achieving financial independence, and the steps you can take to reach this goal.

Financial independence is a state where you have enough assets to support your lifestyle without relying on traditional employment. This means that you have enough money saved up to cover your expenses and can maintain your current lifestyle without relying on a regular paycheck. Achieving financial independence requires a combination of saving, investing, and smart spending habits.

Early retirement, on the other hand, means retiring from traditional employment before the age of 65. Early retirement is becoming increasingly popular as more people are realizing the benefits of leaving the workforce earlier and pursuing other passions or hobbies. However, early retirement is only possible if you have achieved financial independence.

The benefits of achieving financial independence are many. Firstly, it provides you with the freedom to do what you want without worrying about finances. You can choose to pursue your passion, start a business, travel, or simply spend time with loved ones without being tied down to a job. Financial independence also gives you the option to retire early if you choose to do so.

Secondly, achieving financial independence provides you with peace of mind. You no longer have to worry about living paycheck to paycheck or being in debt. You can be confident in your ability to manage your finances and can plan for the future without worrying about unexpected financial setbacks.

Thirdly, achieving financial independence allows you to leave a legacy. You can use your financial resources to support causes you believe in, help your family and friends, or simply leave a positive impact on the world.

Now that we have explored what financial independence and early retirement mean and the benefits of achieving financial independence let's look at the steps you can take to reach this goal.

The first step to achieving financial independence is to create a budget. A budget will help you keep track of your income and expenses and ensure that you are living within your means. By creating a budget, you can identify areas where you can cut back on expenses and redirect those funds towards your savings and investment goals.

The second step is to pay off debt. Debt can be a major obstacle to achieving financial independence. The interest payments on debt can add up quickly and eat into your savings. By paying off debt, you can redirect those funds towards your savings and investment goals.

The third step is to save aggressively. Aim to save at least 20% of your income and invest it in a diversified portfolio of stocks, bonds, and other assets. The key to successful investing is to have a long-term perspective and avoid making emotional decisions.

The fourth step is to live below your means. This means avoiding unnecessary expenses and making smart choices when it comes to spending. For example, you can save money on groceries by buying in bulk or purchasing generic brands. You can also save money on housing by living in a smaller home or in a less expensive neighborhood.

The fifth step is to diversify your income. Having multiple streams of income can help you achieve financial independence faster. This could include starting a side business, investing in rental properties, or pursuing freelance work.

In conclusion, achieving financial independence and early retirement is possible with the right mindset and habits. By creating a budget, paying off debt, saving aggressively, living below your means, and diversifying your income, you can achieve financial independence and have the freedom to retire early if you choose to do so. The key to success is to stay focused on your goals, make smart choices when it comes to spending and investing, and have a long-term perspective

Understanding the FIRE Movement

The FIRE movement, which stands for Financial Independence Retire Early, is a growing trend among individuals seeking to retire early by saving and investing aggressively. This movement has gained a lot of attention in recent years, especially among millennials who are looking to take control of their financial futures.

At its core, the FIRE movement is all about achieving financial independence at an early age. Financial independence means having enough savings and passive income to cover your living expenses without relying on traditional employment. In other words, you could retire early and have the financial freedom to pursue other interests, such as traveling, volunteering, or spending time with family.

The FIRE movement has several core principles that guide its adherents. These principles include:

1. Maximizing Savings: FIRE followers believe in living below their means and saving as much money as possible. They aim to save at least 50% of their income, often by cutting back on unnecessary expenses such as eating out or buying new clothes.

2. Investing Aggressively: To achieve financial independence, FIRE followers invest aggressively in the stock market and other high-yield investments. They aim to generate passive income that can cover their living expenses.

3. Minimizing Debt: FIRE followers try to minimize debt as much as possible, especially high-interest debt like credit cards and personal loans. They may pay off their mortgage early or choose to rent instead of buying a home to minimize debt.

4. Frugal Living: FIRE followers believe in living a frugal lifestyle, avoiding unnecessary purchases and seeking out deals and discounts whenever possible.

While the FIRE movement has gained a lot of attention, it is not without its critics. Some argue that the movement is only accessible to those with high incomes or that it promotes a lifestyle that is not sustainable or fulfilling. Others question the assumption that early retirement is always desirable, arguing that work can provide a sense of purpose and community that is difficult to replace.

Despite these criticisms, many individuals have found the principles of the FIRE movement to be helpful in achieving their financial goals. By focusing on maximizing savings, investing aggressively, minimizing debt, and living frugally, it is possible to achieve financial independence and retire early. However, it is important to remember that everyone's financial situation is unique, and what works for one person may not work for another.

In conclusion, the FIRE movement is a growing trend that seeks to achieve financial independence and retire early through aggressive savings and investing. While it has its critics, the principles of the FIRE movement can be helpful in achieving financial goals and taking control of one's financial future. As with any financial strategy, it is important to consider your unique situation and goals before committing to any particular approach.

Strategies for Achieving Financial Independence

Strategies for Achieving Financial Independence

Achieving financial independence can be a daunting task, but it is a worthy goal to strive towards. Financial independence means having enough money to cover your expenses without relying on a job or other source of income. It gives you the freedom to pursue your passions, take risks, and make choices without worrying about how you will pay your bills. However, reaching this goal requires careful planning, hard work, and discipline. In this essay, we will explore some strategies for achieving financial independence.

Create a budget

The first step towards financial independence is to create a budget. A budget helps you understand your income and expenses, and it allows you to plan your spending and saving accordingly. To create a budget, start by listing all your sources of income and your monthly expenses. Be sure to include everything, from your rent or mortgage payment to your daily cup of coffee. Once you have a clear picture of your finances, you can identify areas where you can cut back and allocate more money towards savings.

Live below your means

Living below your means is one of the most important strategies for achieving financial independence. This means that you should spend less than you earn and avoid taking on debt. You can accomplish this by cutting back on unnecessary expenses, such as eating out or buying new clothes, and by finding ways to save money, such as by cooking at home and buying used items. By living below your means, you can save more money and invest it for the future.

Build an emergency fund

An emergency fund is a crucial component of any financial plan. It is a savings account that you can tap into in case of unexpected expenses or emergencies, such as a job loss or a medical bill. Ideally, your emergency fund should cover three to six months of living expenses. By having an emergency fund, you can avoid going into debt and keep your financial plan on track.

Invest in your future

Investing is a key strategy for achieving financial independence. By investing your money, you can earn a return on your investment and grow your wealth over time. There are many different types of investments, such as stocks, bonds, and real estate, and each has its own risks and rewards. It is important to do your research and choose investments that align with your financial goals and risk tolerance.

Maximize your income

Maximizing your income is another important strategy for achieving financial independence. This can include asking for a raise at work, taking on a side job, or starting a business. By increasing your income, you can save more money and invest more for the future. However, it is important to be mindful of how you spend your extra income and to avoid lifestyle inflation.

Pay off debt

Paying off debt is an essential part of achieving financial independence. Debt can be a major burden on your finances and can prevent you from reaching your goals. By paying off your debt, you can free up more money to save and invest. Start by paying off high-interest debt, such as credit card debt, and work your way towards paying off all your debts.

Be patient

Achieving financial independence takes time and patience. It requires a long-term perspective and a commitment to your financial goals. You may face setbacks along the way, such as a job loss or a market downturn, but it is important to stay focused and continue to work towards your goals. Remember, financial independence is not a quick fix, but a lifelong journey.

Planning for Early Retirement

Planning for early retirement is a dream for many people. It provides the opportunity to enjoy the freedom of not having to work, travel, spend more time with family and pursue other interests that you might not have had time for while working. However, early retirement requires careful planning and preparation, particularly when it comes to saving money. In this essay, we will explore some strategies for planning and saving for early retirement.

The first step in planning for early retirement is to determine how much money you will need to save. This will depend on a variety of factors, including your lifestyle, where you live, and how long you expect to live. It is important to consider not only your basic living expenses but also the expenses you will incur for travel, hobbies, and medical care. You should also factor in inflation, as the cost of living will increase over time.

One way to estimate how much you will need to save is to use a retirement calculator. These tools take into account various factors such as your age, income, savings, and expected investment returns, to help you determine how much you will need to save each year to meet your retirement goals. You can use these calculators to adjust your assumptions and see how different factors can affect your retirement savings.

Once you have an idea of how much you need to save, the next step is to create a plan for achieving your goals. This may involve making changes to your current spending habits to free up money for retirement savings. Some common strategies for saving money include reducing expenses, increasing income, and investing in the stock market.

Reducing expenses can be accomplished in many ways. One way is to downsize your living situation, for example, moving to a smaller house or apartment or living in a lower-cost area. Another way to reduce expenses is to cut back on discretionary spending such as eating out, entertainment, or vacations. You can also consider cutting expenses by negotiating bills and shopping for deals on insurance, utilities, and other recurring expenses.

Increasing your income can be done in several ways as well. You can work more hours or take on a side hustle to earn extra money. If you have skills or expertise in a particular area, you could also consider starting a business or consulting on the side. Another option is to invest in rental properties, which can provide a steady stream of passive income.

Investing in the stock market is another strategy for building wealth and achieving early retirement. Many financial experts recommend a mix of stocks, bonds, and other assets, depending on your risk tolerance and investment goals. You can invest in individual stocks or mutual funds, which are professionally managed portfolios of stocks and other securities.

In addition to these strategies, it is also important to consider the tax implications of early retirement. For example, withdrawing money from a traditional IRA or 401(k) before age 59 1/2 can result in penalties and taxes. However, there are several ways to access retirement funds without penalty, such as through a Roth IRA or 72(t) distributions. It is important to work with a financial advisor or tax professional to determine the best approach for your specific situation.

Finally, it is essential to regularly review and adjust your retirement plan as needed. As your life circumstances change, your retirement needs and goals may also shift. For example, you may need to adjust your savings rate if you experience a job loss or other financial setback. On the other hand, if you receive an unexpected windfall or increase in income, you may be able to accelerate your retirement savings goals.

In conclusion, planning for early retirement requires careful consideration and a long-term strategy. By estimating your retirement needs, creating a plan, and implementing a range of savings strategies, you can work toward achieving your financial goals.

Chapter Twenty-One

Saving Money on Auto Expenses

Owning a car is a necessity for many people, but it can also be a significant expense. In addition to the upfront cost of buying a vehicle, there are ongoing expenses such as fuel, insurance, and maintenance that can quickly add up. Fortunately, there are many ways to save money on auto expenses without sacrificing safety or convenience.

One of the easiest ways to save money on auto expenses is to drive less. If possible, consider carpooling, using public transportation, or walking or biking for short trips. This not only saves money on fuel but also reduces wear and tear on the vehicle, which can lead to lower maintenance costs over time.

Another way to save money on auto expenses is to shop around for the best insurance rates. It's important to have adequate insurance coverage, but that doesn't mean you have to pay top dollar for it. Compare rates from multiple insurance providers to find the best deal, and be sure to ask about discounts for things like safe driving, multiple policies, or installing safety features in your vehicle.

Regular maintenance is essential for keeping your car running smoothly, but it can also be expensive. To save money on maintenance costs, consider doing some basic tasks yourself, such as checking and replacing the air filter, changing the oil, and rotating the tires. Many of these tasks require little more than a few basic tools and some know-how, and there are plenty of online resources and tutorials available to help you get started.

When it comes time for more significant repairs or maintenance, be sure to shop around for the best deal. Don't be afraid to ask for estimates from multiple mechanics or dealerships to compare prices and find the most affordable option. Keep in mind that the cheapest option isn't always the best, and it's worth investing in quality repairs that will last rather than cutting corners to save a few dollars.

One way to save money on auto expenses over the long term is to choose a vehicle that is fuel-efficient and has low maintenance costs. While a hybrid or electric vehicle may be more expensive upfront, the savings in fuel and maintenance costs can add up over time. Similarly, choosing a reliable, well-built vehicle with a good track record for longevity can save you money in the long run by reducing the need for costly repairs.

Finally, consider the cost of financing your vehicle when making a purchase. A longer loan term may result in lower monthly payments, but it also means paying more in interest over time. Similarly, a higher down payment can result in lower monthly payments and less interest over the life of the loan. Be sure to shop around for the best financing rates and terms to ensure that you're getting the best deal possible.

In conclusion, there are many ways to save money on auto expenses without sacrificing safety or convenience. By driving less, shopping around for insurance rates, doing basic maintenance tasks yourself, and choosing a fuel-efficient and low-maintenance vehicle, you can significantly reduce the ongoing costs of owning a car. Additionally, by being mindful of financing terms and shopping around for the best deal, you can save money on the upfront cost of purchasing a vehicle. With a little planning and effort, you can enjoy the benefits of owning a car without breaking the bank.

Buying vs. Leasing: Making the Right Choice

The decision to buy or lease a car can have a significant impact on your finances. While both options have their advantages and disadvantages, it is essential to weigh your options carefully and choose the best one for your situation. In this essay, we will explore the differences between buying and leasing a car and provide some tips to help you make the right choice.

Buying a Car

Buying a car involves paying for the entire cost of the vehicle, either in cash or through financing. If you choose to finance, you will need to make a down payment and pay interest on the loan over a set period, usually between three and six years. Once you have paid off the loan, you own the car outright.

One of the primary advantages of buying a car is that you have complete ownership and control over the vehicle. You can modify it as you see fit, and you are not limited by the terms of a lease agreement. Additionally, once you have paid off the loan, you have a valuable asset that you can sell or trade-in for another vehicle.

On the other hand, buying a car can be expensive upfront, and the payments can be high, depending on the interest rate and the length of the loan. Additionally, as the car gets older, it may require more maintenance and repairs, which can add to the overall cost of ownership.

Leasing a Car

Leasing a car involves paying for the use of the vehicle for a set period, usually two to three years. Unlike buying a car, you do not own the vehicle at the end of the lease agreement. Instead, you return it to the dealership or have the option to buy it at a predetermined price.

Leasing a car can have several advantages, including lower monthly payments, fewer upfront costs, and the ability to drive a new car every few years. Additionally, since leased cars are typically under warranty for the duration of the lease, you may not have to worry about maintenance and repair costs.

However, leasing a car also has some disadvantages. For example, you are limited in how much you can customize the vehicle, and you may be charged additional fees if you exceed the mileage limit set in the lease agreement. Additionally, since you do not own the vehicle, you have no equity in the car, and you are not building up any value for yourself.

Choosing the Right Option

When deciding whether to buy or lease a car, several factors should be taken into account. These include your budget, your driving habits, your need for customization, and your long-term goals.

If you are on a tight budget, leasing may be the best option since it typically involves lower monthly payments than buying. However, if you plan to keep the car for a long time and want to build equity in the vehicle, buying may be the better choice.

Your driving habits are also a crucial factor to consider. If you drive a lot and tend to put many miles on the car each year, leasing may not be the best option since you will likely exceed the mileage limit and incur additional fees. On the other hand, if you only use the car for occasional trips, leasing may be a good choice.

Finally, your need for customization should also be taken into account. If you want to modify the car in any way, buying may be the better option since you own the vehicle and have complete control over it. However, if you do not plan to modify the car, leasing may be a viable option.

Conclusion

In conclusion, buying and leasing a car both have their advantages and disadvantages. When making your decision, it is essential to consider your budget, your driving habits, your need for customization, and your long-term goals. By weighing your options carefully, you can make an informed decision and choose the option that is best

Tips for Saving on Car Insurance

Car insurance is a necessary expense for anyone who drives, but it can be expensive. Fortunately, there are ways to save money on car insurance without sacrificing coverage. Here are some tips for saving on car insurance.

1. Shop Around: One of the best ways to save money on car insurance is to shop around. Don't just settle for the first insurance company you find. Get quotes from several companies and compare them. You may be surprised at how much you can save by switching to a different company.

2. Increase Your Deductible: Your deductible is the amount of money you have to pay out of pocket before your insurance kicks in. If you increase your deductible, your monthly premiums will be lower. Just make sure you can afford to pay the higher deductible if you get into an accident.

3. Bundle Your Insurance: Many insurance companies offer discounts if you have multiple policies with them. For example, you could save money by bundling your car insurance with your homeowners or renters insurance.

4. Maintain Good Credit: Believe it or not, your credit score can affect your car insurance rates. People with good credit scores are generally considered to be less of a risk, so they get lower rates. Make sure you pay your bills on time and keep your credit utilization low to maintain a good credit score.

5. Drive Safely: Your driving record is another factor that can affect your car insurance rates. If you have a history of accidents or traffic violations, you'll pay more for insurance. Drive safely and obey traffic laws to keep your rates low.

6. Take Advantage of Discounts: Many insurance companies offer discounts for things like good driving habits, completing a defensive driving course, or being a member of certain organizations. Ask your insurance company about discounts you may be eligible for.

7. Choose Your Car Wisely: The type of car you drive can also affect your insurance rates. Sports cars and luxury vehicles are generally more expensive to insure than economy cars. If you're in the market for a new car, consider the insurance costs before making a purchase.

8. Opt for Pay-As-You-Go Insurance: Some insurance companies offer pay-as-you-go insurance, which charges you based on the number of miles you drive. If you don't drive very much, this could be a great way to save money on insurance.

9. Review Your Coverage: Finally, review your insurance coverage regularly to make sure you're not paying for more coverage than you need. If you have an older car, for example, you may not need comprehensive coverage.

In conclusion, car insurance is a necessary expense for drivers, but it doesn't have to break the bank. By shopping around, increasing your deductible, bundling your insurance, maintaining good credit, driving safely, taking advantage of discounts, choosing your car wisely, opting for pay-as-you-go insurance, and reviewing your coverage regularly, you can save money on car insurance without sacrificing coverage.

Maintenance and Fuel Efficiency Strategies

1. Saving money on auto expenses can be a daunting task, especially when you rely on your car for daily transportation. However, there are several strategies you can employ to reduce your auto expenses and keep more money in your pocket. In this essay, we will focus on two areas: maintenance and fuel efficiency.

Maintenance

Regular maintenance of your vehicle is key to reducing the frequency of costly repairs and prolonging the life of your car. Here are some tips for keeping your car in good condition without breaking the bank:

Follow the manufacturer's recommended maintenance schedule. Your car manual will include a schedule of recommended maintenance tasks, such as oil changes, tire rotations, and air filter replacements. Following this schedule will help prevent costly repairs down the line.

Check your fluids regularly. Fluids such as oil, coolant, and transmission fluid are essential to your car's performance. Check these fluids regularly and top them up when necessary.

Replace your air filter regularly. A dirty air filter can reduce your car's fuel efficiency, so it's important to replace it regularly. Check your manual for the recommended replacement interval.

Keep your tires properly inflated. Properly inflated tires can improve your car's fuel efficiency and extend the life of your tires. Check your tire pressure regularly and inflate them to the recommended pressure.

Fuel Efficiency

Reducing your fuel consumption is another effective way to save money on auto expenses. Here are some tips for improving your car's fuel efficiency:

Drive conservatively. Aggressive driving, such as speeding and rapid acceleration, can increase your fuel consumption. Try to drive smoothly and avoid sudden movements.

Avoid unnecessary idling. Idling your car consumes fuel without moving your car, so turn off your engine when you're parked or stopped for an extended period.

Use cruise control. Using cruise control on the highway can help maintain a consistent speed and improve your car's fuel efficiency.

Remove excess weight from your car. The more weight your car carries, the more fuel it consumes. Remove any unnecessary items from your car, such as heavy tools or sports equipment.

Keep your car well-maintained. Regular maintenance, such as oil changes and tire rotations, can improve your car's fuel efficiency.

Saving money on auto expenses is a crucial part of managing your personal finances. By employing these strategies, you can reduce your car's maintenance costs and improve its fuel efficiency, saving you money in the long run. Remember to follow your car's maintenance schedule, keep your tires properly inflated, and drive conservatively to maximize your fuel efficiency. With these tips, you can keep your auto expenses under control and keep more money in your pocket.

Chapter Twenty-Two

Side Hustles and Passive Income

Side hustles and passive income streams have become increasingly popular as people look for ways to supplement their income and save more money. Whether you're looking to pay off debt, save for a big purchase, or build wealth, having a side hustle or passive income stream can help you reach your financial goals faster. In this essay, we'll explore what side hustles and passive income are, how they can benefit you, and some examples of popular options.

Side hustles are jobs or businesses that you do outside of your primary source of income. They're a way to earn extra money while still keeping your day job. A side hustle can be anything from selling handmade crafts online to driving for a ride-sharing service to providing freelance services like writing, graphic design, or consulting. The beauty of a side hustle is that it can be tailored to your interests and skills, allowing you to monetize your passions and turn them into a source of income.

Passive income, on the other hand, is money that you earn without actively working for it. It's money that comes in regularly without requiring you to put in continuous effort. Examples of passive income include rental income, investing in stocks or real estate, and creating digital products like ebooks or courses. Passive income requires an initial investment of time and money upfront, but it can pay off in the long run by providing a consistent stream of income.

One of the biggest benefits of having a side hustle or passive income stream is that it can provide financial security. In today's uncertain economy, having multiple streams of income can help you weather unexpected financial storms. If you lose your primary source of income, having a side hustle or passive income stream can provide a cushion until you're able to find another job or replace that income.

Another benefit of having a side hustle or passive income stream is that it can help you reach your financial goals faster. Whether you're looking to pay off debt, save for a down payment on a house, or build up your retirement savings, having extra income can help you get there quicker. Plus, the income from your side hustle or passive income stream can be put directly towards your financial goals, allowing you to make progress even faster.

There are countless options for side hustles and passive income streams, so let's take a look at a few popular choices:

1. Freelancing: If you have a skill like writing, graphic design, or web development, you can offer your services on freelance platforms like Upwork or Fiverr. Freelancing allows you to work on projects that interest you and earn money in the process.

2. Affiliate marketing: If you have a blog or social media following, you can earn money by promoting products and services that align with your audience's interests. Many companies offer affiliate programs that pay a commission for each sale made through your unique affiliate link.

3. Rental income: If you have a spare room in your house or a rental property, you can earn passive income by renting it out on platforms like Airbnb or VRBO.

4. Investing: Investing in stocks, mutual funds, or real estate can provide a source of passive income through dividends or rental income. While investing comes with risks, it can be a powerful tool for building wealth over time.

5. Digital products: If you have expertise in a particular area, you can create digital products like ebooks, courses, or printables to sell online. Once created, these products can continue to generate income with little ongoing effort.

While having a side hustle or passive income stream can be a great way to supplement your income and reach your financial goals, it's important to approach them with a strategic mindset. Make sure your side hustle or passive income stream aligns with your skills, interests, and values.

Identifying Your Skills and Interests

In today's economy, many people are looking for ways to increase their income and save more money. One way to achieve this is by starting a side hustle or exploring passive income opportunities. However, before jumping into any business venture, it is important to identify your skills and interests. This essay will explore the importance of identifying your skills and interests and how it can lead to successful side hustles and passive income streams.

The first step in identifying your skills and interests is to make a list of your passions and hobbies. Consider what you enjoy doing in your free time or what you would do if money wasn't an issue. This list could include anything from writing to baking, from photography to graphic design. The goal is to identify areas in which you already have some expertise or are willing to learn.

Next, it is important to assess your skills and experience. Think about your current job and the skills you use on a daily basis. Also, consider any other experiences or education that you have had that could be useful in a side hustle or passive income stream. For example, if you have experience in marketing or social media, this could be valuable for starting a small business or becoming an influencer.

Once you have a good understanding of your skills and interests, it's time to research different side hustle and passive income opportunities. There are many resources available online, such as blogs, podcasts, and social media groups, that can provide inspiration and guidance for starting a successful business or earning passive income.

When researching opportunities, it's important to consider the time and financial investment required. Some side hustles may require a significant amount of time and money upfront, while others may require only a small investment. It's important to choose an opportunity that fits your lifestyle and budget.

One popular option for earning passive income is through real estate investing. This could involve purchasing a rental property, investing in a real estate fund, or participating in crowdfunding for real estate projects. Real estate investing can be a great way to earn income without actively working, but it does require a significant amount of upfront capital and research.

Another option for earning passive income is through investing in stocks or other financial instruments. This can be done through a variety of online platforms and apps, such as Robinhood, Acorns, or Stash. However, it's important to do your research and understand the risks involved in investing before diving in.

For those interested in starting a side hustle, there are countless options available. Some popular ideas include freelance writing or editing, selling products online, or starting a blog or YouTube channel. Again, it's important to choose an opportunity that aligns with your skills and interests and fits your lifestyle.

In addition to identifying your skills and interests, it's important to have a solid financial plan in place. Starting a side hustle or investing in real estate or stocks can be a great way to earn extra income, but it's also important to budget and save wisely. Make sure you have a good understanding of your monthly expenses and prioritize saving and investing for your future.

In conclusion, identifying your skills and interests is an important step in starting a successful side hustle or earning passive income. By considering your passions and expertise, researching different opportunities, and having a solid financial plan in place, you can find a business venture that aligns with your lifestyle and goals. Whether you're looking to earn extra income or achieve financial independence, there are many options available for those willing to put in the time and effort.

Generating Additional Income Streams

In today's economy, many people are seeking ways to increase their income and improve their financial situation. One popular strategy is to generate additional income streams through side hustles and other means. By diversifying their sources of income, individuals can reduce their reliance on a single job or source of income, and potentially increase their overall earnings. In this essay, we will explore some strategies for generating additional income streams, as well as some considerations to keep in mind when pursuing these opportunities.

The first step in identifying potential income streams is to assess your skills, interests, and resources. What are you good at? What do you enjoy doing? Do you have any assets or resources that could be used to generate income? Some common examples of skills and resources that can be monetized include:

Writing and editing

Graphic design

Photography and videography

Social media management

Tutoring or teaching

Consulting or coaching

Renting out a room or property

Driving for ride-sharing or delivery services

Selling products online

Investing in stocks or real estate

Once you have identified your skills and resources, you can start exploring potential income streams. Some ideas to consider include:

1. Freelancing: If you have skills such as writing, graphic design, or social media management, you can offer your services on freelance platforms such as Upwork, Fiverr, or Freelancer. These platforms allow you to find clients and projects, set your own rates, and work on your own schedule.

2. Online courses: If you have expertise in a particular area, you can create and sell online courses on platforms such as Udemy or Skillshare. This can

be a great way to monetize your knowledge and skills, and potentially earn passive income over time.

3. Affiliate marketing: If you have a blog or social media following, you can earn money by promoting products or services through affiliate marketing. This involves including affiliate links in your content, and earning a commission on any sales that result from those links.

4. Renting out a property: If you have an extra room or property, you can rent it out on platforms such as Airbnb or Vrbo. This can be a great way to generate passive income, especially if you live in a popular tourist destination.

5. Investing: If you have some money to invest, you can potentially earn additional income through stocks, mutual funds, or real estate. However, it's important to remember that investing always carries some level of risk, and it's important to do your research and consult with a financial advisor before making any investment decisions.

While generating additional income can be a great way to improve your financial situation, it's important to keep in mind some potential downsides as well. For example, taking on too many side hustles or freelance projects can lead to burnout and stress. It's important to find a balance between earning additional income and taking care of your physical and mental health.

Another consideration is the impact that additional income may have on your taxes. Depending on the amount of income you generate, you may need to pay additional taxes or make changes to your tax strategy. It's important to consult with a tax professional to ensure that you are staying compliant with all tax regulations.

In conclusion, generating additional income streams can be a great way to improve your financial situation and reach your financial goals. By identifying your skills and resources, exploring potential income streams, and keeping in mind the potential downsides and considerations, you can start building a diversified income portfolio that can help you achieve financial independence and security.

Maximizing Earnings While Minimizing Effort

Maximizing earnings while minimizing effort is a desirable goal for many individuals who are looking to increase their income without taking on additional stress or responsibility. With the rise of technology and the gig economy, there are now more opportunities than ever to earn extra income in a flexible and low-effort manner. In this essay, we will explore some effective strategies for maximizing earnings while minimizing effort.

Passive income streams

One of the most effective ways to generate income without expending much effort is by creating passive income streams. Passive income is money earned without active involvement, such as through rental income, investment dividends, or online courses. While creating a passive income stream may require initial effort, such as investing in a rental property or creating an online course, once established, the income generated requires minimal effort to maintain. This can be a great option for those looking to earn extra income without sacrificing their free time.

Online surveys and focus groups

Online surveys and focus groups are another low-effort way to earn extra income. Companies are always looking for feedback on their products and services, and they are willing to pay for it. Websites such as Survey Junkie and Swagbucks offer opportunities to earn money by taking surveys or participating in focus groups. While the income generated from online surveys and focus groups may not be substantial, it can be a good way to earn a little extra income in your spare time.

Rent out your space

Another way to generate income without much effort is by renting out your space. If you have a spare room or an entire property, you can rent it out on websites such as Airbnb or Vrbo. These platforms allow you to list your space for rent, and renters can book it for short-term stays. While there may be some initial effort involved in preparing your space for renters, once it is set up, the income generated requires minimal effort.

Affiliate marketing

Affiliate marketing is a low-effort way to earn income through referrals. This involves promoting products or services and earning a commission for each sale made through your referral link. Affiliate marketing can be done through social media, blogs, or websites. This strategy requires some initial effort to build an audience and establish relationships with companies, but once it is set up, it can be a good source of passive income.

Sell digital products

If you have a skill or talent, such as graphic design or writing, you can create digital products to sell online. Websites such as Etsy and Gumroad allow you to sell digital products such as ebooks, printables, and templates. Once you create the product, you can sell it repeatedly, generating income without much additional effort.

Maximizing earnings while minimizing effort is a desirable goal for many individuals. There are now more opportunities than ever to earn extra income in a flexible and low-effort manner. Strategies such as creating passive income streams, participating in online surveys and focus groups, renting out your space, affiliate marketing, and selling digital products can all be effective ways to increase your income without sacrificing your free time. With some initial effort and creativity, it is possible to create a steady stream of passive income and achieve financial independence.

Ideas for possible side hustles:

Chapter Twenty-Three

Saving Money for Charitable Giving and Philanthropy

- Freelance writing: Write for blogs or websites for pay.
- Graphic design: Create logos or designs for businesses.
- Social media management: Manage social media accounts for businesses.
- Virtual assistant: Provide administrative or organizational support remotely.
- Tutoring: Offer tutoring services for a specific subject or age group.
- Pet-sitting or dog-walking: Care for pets while owners are away.
- House-sitting: Watch homes while owners are on vacation.
- Personal shopping: Shop for others and charge a fee for your services.
- Photography: Take photos for events or businesses.
- Event planning: Plan and organize events for individuals or businesses.
- Landscaping: Offer landscaping or gardening services.

- Cleaning services: Offer cleaning services for homes or businesses.
- Handyman services: Offer handyman services for home repairs and maintenance.
- Personal training: Offer fitness training or coaching services.
- Music lessons: Offer music lessons for a specific instrument or voice.
- Translation services: Offer translation services for businesses or individuals.
- Voice acting: Provide voice-over services for commercials or videos.
- Podcasting: Create and produce your own podcast for sponsorship or advertising revenue.
- DJ services: Offer DJ services for events or parties.
- Meal prep or catering: Prepare meals or cater for events.
- Personal chef: Cook for individuals or families on a regular basis.
- Car detailing: Offer car detailing services for individuals or businesses.
- Delivery services: Offer delivery services for restaurants or stores.
- Errand running: Offer errand running services for busy individuals.
- Personal shopping: Shop for individuals and charge a fee for your services.

- Cleaning services: Offer cleaning services for homes or businesses.
- Mobile car washing: Wash cars for individuals or businesses.
- Social media influencer: Build a following on social media and earn money through sponsored posts and partnerships.
- Voiceover artist: Provide voice-over services for commercials or videos.
- Survey taking: Take online surveys for pay.
- Mystery shopping: Shop at stores and report on customer service and overall experience.
- Data entry: Provide data entry services for businesses.
- Online tutoring: Offer tutoring services online.
- Greeting card making: Create and sell handmade greeting cards.
- Sell crafts on Etsy: Sell handmade crafts on Etsy.
- Blogging: Create and monetize your own blog.
- Affiliate marketing: Promote products or services and earn a commission on sales.
- Online coaching: Offer coaching services for personal or professional development.
- Transcription: Provide transcription services for businesses or individuals.
- Online teaching: Teach classes or workshops online.

- Online course creation: Create and sell online courses on a specific topic.
- Social media advertising: Create and manage social media ad campaigns for businesses.
- Personal shopping: Shop for individuals and charge a fee for your services.
- Cleaning services: Offer cleaning services for homes or businesses.
- Mobile app development: Develop and sell mobile apps.
- E-commerce: Sell products online through your own website or a platform like Amazon.
- Affiliate marketing: Promote products or services and earn a commission on sales.
- Voice acting: Provide voice-over services for commercials or videos.
- Video editing: Edit videos for businesses or individuals.
- Website design: Design and build websites for businesses or individuals.

Saving Money for Charitable Giving and Philanthropy

Saving money for charitable giving and philanthropy is a noble endeavor that can have a significant impact on the lives of those in need. By making a conscious effort to save money, you can set aside funds to donate to causes that are important to you. However, saving money for charitable giving requires a thoughtful and intentional approach to ensure that your contributions have the greatest possible impact.

The first step in saving money for charitable giving is to identify causes that are important to you. Consider what issues you feel most passionate about, whether it's helping the less fortunate, promoting education, protecting the environment, or advancing medical research. Once you have identified the causes you want to support, you can research reputable charitable organizations that align with your values and goals.

One way to maximize your contributions is to give to charities that have a track record of efficiency and effectiveness. Look for organizations that have a low overhead and are transparent about how they allocate their resources. Websites like Charity Navigator can provide valuable information about a charity's financial health, governance, and transparency, allowing you to make an informed decision about where to donate your money.

Another way to maximize the impact of your charitable giving is to make a long-term commitment to supporting a particular cause or organization. Instead of making a one-time donation, consider setting up a recurring donation or establishing a donor-advised fund that can provide ongoing support to the charities you care about. By making a long-term commitment, you can help provide stable funding for programs and initiatives that make a real difference in people's lives.

Saving money for charitable giving requires discipline and consistency. One way to stay on track is to establish a budget that includes a line item for charitable giving. Just as you set aside money for groceries, housing, and transportation, you can set aside a portion of your income each month for charitable contributions. This can help you stay focused on your goal of supporting causes that are important to you, and can also help you avoid the temptation to spend money on non-essential items.

There are also a variety of strategies you can use to increase the amount of money you are able to save for charitable giving. For example, you could look for ways to reduce your expenses, such as by cutting back on dining out or canceling unused subscriptions. You could also consider taking on a side hustle or freelance work to earn extra income that can be earmarked for charitable giving.

In addition to monetary contributions, there are other ways to support charitable causes that don't require significant financial resources. For example, you could volunteer your time and expertise to organizations that align with your values. You could also consider donating goods or services, such as clothing or professional services, that can help support the mission of a particular charity.

When it comes to charitable giving, it's important to approach the process with intentionality and thoughtfulness. By taking the time to identify the causes that matter most to you, researching reputable charities, and establishing a plan for ongoing contributions, you can maximize the impact of your donations and make a meaningful difference in the lives of others.

Aligning Your Values with Your Savings Goals

Saving money is an important aspect of financial planning, but it can often feel like a chore. It's difficult to consistently set aside a portion of your income when there are so many other expenses and bills to pay. However, by aligning your values with your savings goals, you can not only make saving money easier, but also feel more fulfilled in your financial planning.

So, what exactly does it mean to align your values with your savings goals? Essentially, it's about creating a financial plan that reflects your personal beliefs and priorities. For example, if you're passionate about the environment, you might focus on saving money by reducing your energy consumption, buying energy-efficient appliances, and supporting eco-friendly companies. Or, if you value giving back to your community, you might prioritize donating to charities or volunteering your time instead of spending money on expensive vacations or gadgets.

Here are some strategies for aligning your values with your savings goals:

Identify your values and priorities

The first step is to identify your values and priorities. What matters most to you in life? What are your long-term goals? Take some time to reflect on these questions and write down your answers. This will help you determine what you want to focus on in your financial planning.

Set specific savings goals

Once you know your values and priorities, it's time to set specific savings goals. For example, if you're passionate about traveling, you might set a goal to save a certain amount of money each month for a future trip. If you're focused on paying off debt, you might set a goal to put a specific amount towards debt repayment each month.

Find ways to align your spending with your values

One of the biggest challenges of saving money is avoiding temptation to spend on things that don't align with your values. To help overcome this challenge, find ways to align your spending with your values. For example, if you value supporting small businesses, make an effort to shop at local stores instead of big chain retailers. If you're passionate about health and wellness, invest in a gym membership or healthy meal delivery service instead of spending money on fast food.

Look for opportunities to save while also giving back

Another way to align your values with your savings goals is to look for opportunities to save money while also giving back. For example, if you're passionate about education, you might consider donating to a scholarship fund or supporting a local school. You could also look for volunteer opportunities that align with your values, such as tutoring or mentoring programs.

Make conscious decisions about your investments

Investing is a key component of long-term financial planning, and it's important to make conscious decisions about where you're investing your money. If you're passionate about social or environmental causes, consider investing in socially responsible funds or companies that align with your values. You could also look for investment opportunities that support specific causes, such as renewable energy or affordable housing.

Continually reassess and adjust your plan

Finally, it's important to continually reassess and adjust your financial plan as your values and priorities change. Life is unpredictable, and your financial goals may shift over time. By regularly reviewing your plan and making adjustments as needed, you can ensure that your savings goals always align with your values.

In conclusion, aligning your values with your savings goals is an effective way to make financial planning more fulfilling and sustainable. By focusing on what matters most to you in life and finding ways to save money that align with those values, you can create a financial plan that is both personally and financially rewarding.

Smart Giving Strategies for Maximum Impact

Giving to others is an act of kindness that can bring us happiness and a sense of fulfillment. However, charitable giving does not have to mean breaking the bank. It is possible to make a significant impact even with a limited budget. In this essay, we will explore smart giving strategies that can help maximize the impact of charitable giving while also saving money.

The first step in smart giving is to identify causes or organizations that align with your values and interests. This can be done through research or by asking for recommendations from friends and family. Once you have identified a few causes or organizations, it is important to do some due diligence to ensure that they are legitimate and use donations effectively.

One strategy for maximizing the impact of charitable giving is to focus on organizations that have a high impact-to-cost ratio. These organizations are able to do more with less and can make a big difference with even small donations. For example, there are several organizations that provide meals to those in need for just a few dollars per meal. By donating to these organizations, you can provide many meals with a small donation.

Another strategy for smart giving is to donate to organizations that have matching programs. These programs match donations made by individuals, effectively doubling the impact of each donation. Some companies also have matching programs, so it is worth checking if your employer offers this benefit.

It is also important to consider the tax benefits of charitable giving. Donations made to qualified organizations can be deducted on your tax return, which can help reduce your tax bill. However, it is important to keep accurate records and obtain receipts for all donations in order to take advantage of these deductions.

In addition to monetary donations, there are other ways to give back that can also save money. Volunteering time and skills can be a valuable way to contribute to an organization without spending money. This can also provide opportunities to learn new skills or gain experience in a particular field.

Another way to give back is through in-kind donations. This involves donating goods or services rather than cash. For example, you could donate gently used clothing or household items to a local charity. This not only helps the organization but also reduces waste by keeping items out of landfills.

It is important to remember that charitable giving does not have to be limited to financial donations. There are many ways to give back that can also help save money. By identifying causes or organizations that align with your values and interests, doing some due diligence, and considering different giving strategies, you can make a significant impact while also saving money.

In conclusion, smart giving involves identifying causes or organizations that align with your values, doing some research to ensure that they use donations effectively, and considering different giving strategies that can help maximize the impact of charitable giving while also saving money. By incorporating these strategies into your giving habits, you can make a significant impact on the causes that matter to you while also achieving your savings goals.

Tax Benefits and Considerations

When it comes to saving money, taking advantage of tax benefits and considerations can be a powerful tool. By understanding the various tax laws and regulations, individuals can reduce their tax liability and keep more of their hard-earned money in their pockets. In this essay, we will explore some of the tax benefits and considerations that can help individuals save money.

One of the most common ways to save on taxes is by contributing to a retirement account. Retirement accounts, such as 401(k)s and individual retirement accounts (IRAs), allow individuals to save money for retirement while also receiving tax benefits. Contributions to these accounts are tax-deductible, meaning that they reduce an individual's taxable income. In addition, the money in these accounts grows tax-free until it is withdrawn in retirement. This can result in significant savings over the long-term.

Another tax benefit to consider is the home mortgage interest deduction. For those who own a home and have a mortgage, the interest paid on the mortgage is deductible on their tax return. This can result in significant savings, particularly for those with large mortgages. In addition, individuals can also deduct property taxes paid on their home.

For those who are self-employed or own a small business, there are several tax benefits to take advantage of. One of the most significant is the ability to deduct business expenses. This can include expenses such as office rent, supplies, and equipment. In addition, self-employed individuals can deduct contributions to a Simplified Employee Pension (SEP) plan or a solo 401(k) plan.

Another tax benefit to consider is the child tax credit. This credit provides a tax credit of up to $2,000 per child under the age of 17. In addition, there is also a child and dependent care credit that can provide a credit for a portion of child care expenses. These credits can significantly reduce an individual's tax liability and provide valuable savings.

One consideration to keep in mind when it comes to taxes is the alternative minimum tax (AMT). The AMT is a separate tax system that was designed to ensure that individuals with high income and significant deductions still pay a minimum amount of tax. However, the AMT can be complex and may result in individuals paying more in taxes than they would under the regular tax system. It is important to consult with a tax professional to understand how the AMT may impact your tax liability.

Another consideration when it comes to taxes is the timing of income and deductions. By strategically timing when income is received and when deductions are taken, individuals can reduce their tax liability. For example, if an individual expects to earn a large bonus at the end of the year, they may be able to defer it until the following year to reduce their tax liability for the current year.

Finally, it is important to be aware of tax scams and fraud. There are many scams that target individuals during tax season, such as phishing scams and fake IRS calls. It is important to be vigilant and protect yourself from these scams.

In conclusion, there are many tax benefits and considerations that can help individuals save money. From contributing to a retirement account to taking advantage of deductions and credits, individuals can reduce their tax liability and keep more of their hard-earned money. It is important to consult with a tax professional and stay informed about tax laws and regulations to make the most of these opportunities.

Chapter Twenty-Four

Overcoming Common Savings Obstacles

Saving money is an important aspect of personal finance, but many people find it difficult to save regularly or consistently. There are a number of common obstacles that can make saving seem like an insurmountable challenge, from living paycheck to paycheck to dealing with unexpected expenses. However, with the right strategies and mindset, it is possible to overcome these obstacles and build a strong foundation for financial stability.

One of the most common obstacles to saving is simply not having enough money to spare. If you are living paycheck to paycheck, it can be difficult to set aside money for savings, especially if unexpected expenses arise. In this situation, the first step is to evaluate your expenses and see if there are any areas where you can cut back. This might mean looking for cheaper alternatives for things like groceries, transportation, or entertainment.

Another strategy for overcoming the paycheck to paycheck cycle is to find ways to increase your income. This might mean taking on a part-time job or freelance work, or asking for a raise or promotion at your current job. It may also mean starting a side business or investing in stocks or other assets that generate passive income.

Another common obstacle to saving is dealing with unexpected expenses. Whether it's a car repair, medical bill, or home repair, unexpected expenses can quickly eat into your savings and leave you feeling discouraged. To overcome this challenge, it is important to have an emergency fund in place. This can be a separate savings account or a line of credit that you can access in case of an emergency.

To build up your emergency fund, start by setting a goal for how much you want to save. This might be three to six months' worth of living expenses, or a specific dollar amount. Then, set up a savings plan to automatically transfer money into your emergency fund each month. This way, you can build up your savings over time without even thinking about it.

Another common obstacle to saving is the temptation to spend money on things you don't really need. Whether it's impulse buys or keeping up with the latest trends, unnecessary spending can quickly eat into your savings. To overcome this challenge, it is important to be mindful of your spending habits and make a conscious effort to prioritize saving.

One strategy for avoiding unnecessary spending is to create a budget and stick to it. This means tracking your expenses and income, and setting aside a specific amount each month for savings. It may also mean cutting back on discretionary spending, like eating out or buying new clothes.

Another strategy for avoiding unnecessary spending is to focus on experiences rather than things. Instead of buying a new outfit or gadget, consider spending money on a trip or activity that you can enjoy with friends or family. This not only helps you save money, but it also creates memories that can last a lifetime.

Finally, it is important to have the right mindset when it comes to saving. Many people view saving as a chore or a sacrifice, but it can also be a source of empowerment and freedom. By prioritizing saving and investing in your future, you are creating a sense of financial security that can help you weather any storm.

To cultivate a positive mindset around saving, it can be helpful to set specific goals and celebrate small victories along the way. This might mean setting a goal to save a certain amount each month, or to pay off a specific debt. When you reach these goals, take time to celebrate your progress and acknowledge your hard work.

In conclusion, saving money can be a challenging task, but it is essential for long-term financial stability. By identifying common obstacles and developing strategies to overcome them, you can build a strong foundation for your financial future. Whether you are dealing with unexpected expenses, living paycheck to paycheck, or struggling with unnecessary spending, there are steps you can take to prioritize saving and achieve your financial goals.

Dealing with Unexpected Expenses

Unexpected expenses are a part of life, and they can happen to anyone at any time. These expenses can range from a medical emergency to a car breakdown or a home repair. Such expenses can quickly deplete your savings account and leave you in a difficult financial situation. However, there are ways to deal with unexpected expenses and minimize their impact on your finances.

The first step to dealing with unexpected expenses is to have an emergency fund. An emergency fund is a separate savings account that you set up specifically for unexpected expenses. Ideally, your emergency fund should have at least three to six months' worth of living expenses. This will ensure that you have enough money to cover any unexpected expenses without having to dip into your regular savings or retirement accounts.

If you don't already have an emergency fund, start setting aside some money each month until you reach your goal. You can also consider automating your savings by setting up an automatic transfer from your checking account to your emergency fund. This way, you won't even have to think about it.

Once you have an emergency fund in place, the next step is to prioritize your expenses. When you're faced with unexpected expenses, it can be tempting to try to pay for everything at once. However, this can quickly lead to a financial burden that is difficult to overcome.

Instead, prioritize your expenses based on their urgency and importance. For example, if your car breaks down, it may be more urgent to get it fixed than it is to take a vacation or buy new clothes. By prioritizing your expenses, you can ensure that you're using your money wisely and not putting yourself into more debt.

If you don't have enough money in your emergency fund to cover the unexpected expenses, consider other options for financing. For example, you may be able to take out a personal loan or use a credit card with a low interest rate. However, it's important to only use these options if you're confident that you can pay them back in a timely manner.

Another option is to negotiate with your creditors or service providers. For example, if you're facing a medical bill that you can't afford to pay, you may be able to negotiate a payment plan with your healthcare provider. This can help you spread out the cost of the bill over several months, making it more manageable.

Finally, it's important to learn from unexpected expenses and adjust your budget accordingly. Review your spending habits and see if there are areas where you can cut back to make room for unexpected expenses. For example, you may be able to reduce your entertainment budget or cut back on eating out to free up some money for your emergency fund.

In conclusion, unexpected expenses can be stressful and overwhelming, but they don't have to ruin your financial situation. By having an emergency fund, prioritizing your expenses, and considering other financing options, you can deal with unexpected expenses in a way that minimizes their impact on your finances. Remember to always adjust your budget and learn from your experiences so that you're better prepared for the next unexpected expense that comes your way.

Navigating Financial Challenges and Setbacks

Navigating Financial Challenges and Setbacks

Financial challenges and setbacks are a common experience for many people. Whether it's unexpected expenses, a job loss, or a sudden reduction in income, these setbacks can cause stress and anxiety. However, with the right strategies and mindset, it's possible to navigate these challenges and come out stronger on the other side. In this essay, we'll explore some tips and strategies for overcoming financial setbacks.

The first step to overcoming a financial setback is to assess your current situation. This means taking a close look at your income, expenses, debts, and savings. You should create a budget to help you better understand where your money is going and identify areas where you can cut back. This will help you get a better understanding of how much you need to cover your expenses and debts and how much you can realistically put aside for savings and emergencies.

Once you have a clear picture of your financial situation, you can start taking action to address any immediate challenges. This might mean cutting back on non-essential expenses, finding ways to increase your income, or exploring options for debt consolidation or restructuring. If you have debts that are causing you significant stress and anxiety, it may be worth speaking with a financial counselor or debt specialist to explore your options for managing them.

It's also important to start building up an emergency fund to prepare for future financial challenges. This can help provide a safety net for unexpected expenses or income reductions. Financial experts recommend having at least three to six months' worth of living expenses saved up in an emergency fund. While this may seem daunting, starting small and consistently saving even a small amount each month can help you build up your emergency fund over time.

Another important strategy for navigating financial setbacks is to prioritize your debts and expenses. This means focusing on paying off high-interest debts first, such as credit card debt, while making minimum payments on lower-interest debts like student loans or mortgages. You can also explore options for negotiating lower interest rates or payment plans with your creditors.

In addition to these strategies, it's important to adopt a positive mindset when it comes to finances. This means focusing on the things you can control and taking action to improve your situation, rather than dwelling on things you can't control. It also means being patient and persistent, as overcoming financial setbacks takes time and effort.

One helpful mindset shift is to focus on opportunities rather than limitations. This means looking for creative ways to increase your income or reduce your expenses, rather than feeling limited by your current situation. For example, you might explore options for freelancing or starting a small business to supplement your income, or find ways to reduce your energy bills by making your home more energy-efficient.

Finally, it's important to seek support when navigating financial setbacks. This might mean talking to a trusted friend or family member, seeking guidance from a financial advisor or counselor, or joining a support group for people going through similar challenges. It's important to remember that you're not alone in your struggles, and there are many resources and people who can help.

In conclusion, financial setbacks can be challenging, but with the right mindset and strategies, it's possible to overcome them. By assessing your current situation, taking action to address immediate challenges, building up an emergency fund, prioritizing your debts and expenses, adopting a positive mindset, and seeking support, you can navigate these challenges and come out stronger on the other side. Remember, small steps over time can lead to big improvements in your financial situation.

Staying Motivated and Committed to Your Savings Goals

Staying motivated and committed to your savings goals can be challenging, especially when it seems like there are endless expenses to worry about. However, with the right mindset and tools, it is possible to stay on track and achieve financial success.

One of the first steps in staying motivated is to set clear and achievable savings goals. These goals should be specific, measurable, and time-bound. For example, instead of setting a general goal to "save more money," try setting a specific goal to save $500 per month for the next six months. Having a clear and achievable goal gives you something to work towards and helps you stay motivated.

Another way to stay motivated is to create a visual representation of your progress. This can be done by using a savings tracker, which allows you to see your progress over time. It can be incredibly motivating to see your savings grow and to see how far you've come since you started. Additionally, regularly reviewing your progress can help you identify areas where you may be overspending or where you can cut back to save even more.

It's important to remember that setbacks and unexpected expenses will inevitably occur. When this happens, it's important to remain focused on your long-term goals and not let a setback derail your progress. One way to do this is to have an emergency fund in place. This can help you cover unexpected expenses without having to dip into your savings or go into debt.

Another way to stay motivated is to surround yourself with like-minded individuals. This can be done by joining online communities or support groups that focus on saving money and achieving financial goals. These groups can provide you with encouragement, advice, and motivation when you need it most.

One of the most effective ways to stay motivated is to celebrate your successes along the way. Whether it's treating yourself to a small reward after achieving a savings goal or simply acknowledging your progress, taking time to celebrate can help keep you motivated and committed to your goals.

In addition to staying motivated, it's important to stay committed to your savings goals. This can be done by creating a budget and sticking to it. A budget can help you identify areas where you may be overspending and can help you create a plan to reduce expenses and increase savings. Additionally, regularly reviewing your budget can help you stay on track and identify areas where you may need to make adjustments.

Another way to stay committed is to automate your savings. This can be done by setting up automatic transfers from your checking account to your savings account on a regular basis. By automating your savings, you can ensure that you are consistently putting money towards your goals without having to think about it.

It's also important to be mindful of your spending habits. This can be done by tracking your expenses and identifying areas where you may be overspending. By being mindful of your spending, you can identify areas where you can cut back and redirect those funds towards your savings goals.

In conclusion, staying motivated and committed to your savings goals requires a combination of mindset and tools. By setting clear and achievable goals, creating a visual representation of your progress, having an emergency fund in place, surrounding yourself with like-minded individuals, celebrating your successes, creating a budget and sticking to it, automating your savings, and being mindful of your spending habits, you can stay on track and achieve financial success.

Quick tips:

Chapter Twenty-Five

Financial Wellness and Mental Health

- Identify your obstacles: Pinpoint the specific obstacles that are preventing you from saving.
- Create a budget: Start by creating a budget to help you better manage your finances.
- Prioritize saving: Make saving a priority by setting a specific savings goal and sticking to it.
- Cut unnecessary expenses: Identify and cut out any unnecessary expenses that are preventing you from saving.
- Automate your savings: Set up automatic transfers to a savings account to make saving a habit.
- Increase your income: Look for ways to increase your income, such as taking on a side hustle or asking for a raise.
- Reduce debt: Pay off debt to free up more money for saving.
- Avoid impulse purchases: Resist the urge to make impulse purchases and stick to your budget.
- Use coupons and discounts: Use coupons and discounts to save money on necessary purchases.

- Track your spending: Keep track of your spending to identify areas where you can cut back.
- Use cash: Use cash instead of credit cards to help limit your spending.
- Set up a rainy day fund: Create an emergency fund to help cover unexpected expenses.
- Stay motivated: Stay motivated by regularly reviewing your progress and celebrating milestones.
- Find an accountability partner: Find someone to hold you accountable for your savings goals.
- Avoid comparison: Avoid comparing yourself to others and focus on your own financial situation.
- Take advantage of employer benefits: Take advantage of employer benefits, such as a 401(k) match or employee stock purchase plan.
- Avoid high-interest debt: Avoid high-interest debt, such as credit card debt, that can hinder your savings efforts.
- Negotiate bills: Negotiate bills, such as cable or phone bills, to reduce your monthly expenses.
- Plan for large expenses: Plan ahead for large expenses, such as vacations or home repairs, to avoid dipping into savings.
- Use a savings app: Use a savings app to help you track your progress and stay motivated.
- Avoid lifestyle inflation: Avoid increasing your spending as your

income increases to maintain your savings goals.

- Look for free activities: Look for free or low-cost activities to enjoy instead of expensive entertainment.
- Use a cash-back credit card: Use a cash-back credit card to earn rewards on necessary purchases.
- Avoid unnecessary fees: Avoid unnecessary fees, such as ATM fees or late payment fees, to save money.
- Shop around for insurance: Shop around for insurance to find the best rates and save money.
- Use a financial planner: Use a financial planner to help you create a long-term savings plan.
- Avoid payday loans: Avoid payday loans and other high-interest loans that can harm your finances.
- Avoid lifestyle creep: Avoid increasing your spending as your income increases to maintain your savings goals.
- Take advantage of tax breaks: Take advantage of tax breaks, such as retirement account contributions, to save money on taxes.
- Stay disciplined: Stay disciplined and committed to your savings goals, even if it means making sacrifices in the short-term.

Financial wellness is an important aspect of overall well-being. When we are financially secure, we can enjoy a better quality of life, feel more in control of our future, and have the resources to pursue our dreams and aspirations. However, the impact of financial stress on mental health is often overlooked. In this essay, we will discuss the importance of financial wellness in relation to mental health and strategies for achieving both.

Financial stress can have a profound impact on mental health. It can lead to anxiety, depression, and a sense of helplessness. When individuals are struggling to make ends meet, they may feel overwhelmed and unable to manage their financial situation. This can lead to feelings of shame, guilt, and a sense of failure. Additionally, financial stress can cause strain on relationships, leading to tension and conflict between partners or family members.

To address the link between financial wellness and mental health, it is important to adopt strategies that promote both. The following are some strategies that can help individuals achieve financial wellness while also supporting mental health.

1. Create a budget: One of the most important steps in achieving financial wellness is to create a budget. This allows individuals to track their income and expenses and make adjustments as needed. By having a clear understanding of their financial situation, individuals can feel more in control and empowered.

2. Build an emergency fund: Having an emergency fund can provide peace of mind and security in times of financial stress. This fund can be used to cover unexpected expenses, such as medical bills or car repairs, without having to rely on credit cards or loans.

3. Seek professional help: For individuals who are struggling with significant financial stress or mental health concerns, seeking professional help can be beneficial. Financial advisors, therapists, or counselors can provide guidance and support in managing financial stress and improving mental health.

4. Practice self-care: It is important to prioritize self-care when dealing with financial stress. This can include engaging in activities that bring joy, such as exercise or hobbies, practicing mindfulness and meditation, and connecting with supportive friends and family members.

5. Identify values and priorities: When individuals have a clear understanding of their values and priorities, they can make intentional choices about how to allocate their resources. This can help individuals feel more aligned with their goals and purpose, leading to a sense of fulfillment and satisfaction.

6. Avoid comparing yourself to others: Social comparison can be a significant source of financial stress. By avoiding the trap of comparing oneself to others, individuals can focus on their own goals and progress, leading to a sense of accomplishment and motivation.

7. Practice gratitude: Gratitude can be a powerful tool in promoting both financial wellness and mental health. By focusing on what is already present in one's life, individuals can cultivate a sense of abundance and contentment, reducing the impact of financial stress on mental health.

In conclusion, financial wellness and mental health are closely linked. By adopting strategies that support both, individuals can achieve greater well-being and enjoy a more fulfilling life. Whether it is creating a budget, building an emergency fund, seeking professional help, practicing self-care, identifying values and priorities, avoiding social comparison, or practicing gratitude, there are many ways to achieve financial wellness and promote mental health.

Recognizing the Emotional Impact of Money

Money is not just a financial resource; it carries significant emotional weight. The way we think about and handle money has a profound impact on our mental and emotional well-being. The relationship between money and emotions is complex, and understanding it is crucial for achieving financial wellness.

One of the most common emotional responses to money is anxiety. Many people experience financial stress due to debt, limited resources, or uncertain economic conditions. This stress can lead to a range of physical and emotional symptoms, including headaches, sleep disturbances, depression, and anxiety.

One way to manage financial anxiety is to create a budget and stick to it. Having a clear understanding of income, expenses, and financial goals can help alleviate some of the uncertainty and stress associated with money. Budgeting can also provide a sense of control and empowerment, which can positively impact mental health.

Another emotional response to money is guilt. People may feel guilty for overspending, not saving enough, or indulging in luxury items. This guilt can lead to negative self-talk and undermine self-esteem. However, it is important to remember that everyone makes financial mistakes, and the key is to learn from them and move forward.

To overcome feelings of guilt, it is helpful to practice self-compassion. Instead of berating oneself for financial mistakes, one can acknowledge the mistake and focus on the positive steps taken to rectify it. It is also important to remember that money does not define a person's worth or value.

Money can also trigger feelings of shame. Shame is often associated with societal expectations and perceptions of financial success. People may feel ashamed of their financial status, especially if it does not align with societal standards. This shame can lead to feelings of isolation, low self-esteem, and depression.

To overcome financial shame, it is essential to acknowledge that societal standards of success do not necessarily reflect personal values and priorities. It is important to set individual financial goals that align with personal values and to celebrate small successes along the way.

Money can also trigger feelings of fear. People may fear losing their financial stability or not having enough money to meet their basic needs. This fear can lead to avoidance of financial tasks, which can worsen financial stress and anxiety.

To overcome financial fear, it is helpful to seek support and guidance from trusted sources, such as financial advisors, counselors, or trusted friends and family members. It is also important to educate oneself about personal finance and to take small steps towards financial security, such as creating an emergency fund or paying off debt.

In conclusion, understanding the emotional impact of money is crucial for achieving financial wellness. Money is not just a financial resource, but it also carries significant emotional weight. By acknowledging and addressing emotional responses to money, individuals can manage financial stress and anxiety, increase self-compassion, and align personal financial goals with personal values and priorities.

Managing Stress and Anxiety Related to Finances

Managing Stress and Anxiety Related to Finances

Money is an essential part of our lives. It is the means by which we purchase our necessities, pay our bills, and enjoy our leisure activities. However, for many people, money is also a source of stress and anxiety. Whether it's the fear of not having enough, the worry of not being able to pay bills on time, or the pressure to save for the future, financial concerns can take a significant toll on our mental health. In this essay, we will discuss some strategies for managing stress and anxiety related to finances.

One of the most effective ways to manage financial stress is to take control of your finances. This means setting up a budget and sticking to it. Knowing where your money is going and having a plan for how to spend it can help alleviate some of the uncertainty and anxiety related to finances. To create a budget, start by tracking your expenses for a few months to get an accurate picture of your spending habits. Then, identify areas where you can cut back and create a plan for how to allocate your funds.

Another strategy for managing financial stress is to build an emergency fund. An emergency fund is a savings account that is used to cover unexpected expenses such as car repairs, medical bills, or job loss. Having an emergency fund can help reduce the anxiety that comes with unexpected expenses because you know that you have a safety net to fall back on. Experts recommend having at least three to six months' worth of living expenses saved in an emergency fund.

When it comes to managing stress and anxiety related to finances, it's important to be mindful of your spending habits. Overspending can lead to debt, which can create a vicious cycle of stress and anxiety. To avoid overspending, try to make mindful purchasing decisions. Ask yourself if you really need the item you are considering purchasing and if it fits into your budget. If not, it's better to wait until you can afford it rather than taking on debt.

Another way to manage financial stress is to seek professional help. Financial advisors and credit counselors can provide valuable advice and support for managing finances. They can help you create a budget, develop a debt repayment plan, and provide tips for saving money. Additionally, they can help you understand the complex world of finance and provide guidance on making sound investment decisions.

In addition to seeking professional help, it's important to communicate with your loved ones about financial concerns. Money is often a sensitive topic, but talking about it openly and honestly with your spouse, partner, or family members can help reduce stress and anxiety. It's important to work together to create a plan for managing finances that works for everyone.

Another way to manage financial stress is to practice self-care. Financial stress can take a significant toll on mental health, so it's important to take care of yourself. Exercise, meditation, and getting enough sleep can all help reduce stress and anxiety related to finances. Additionally, it's important to take time for yourself to do the things you enjoy. This can help you recharge and feel more positive about your financial situation.

Finally, it's important to remember that managing financial stress takes time and effort. It's not something that can be fixed overnight. However, by taking steps to manage your finances, seek professional help, communicate with loved ones, and practice self-care, you can reduce stress and anxiety related to finances and improve your overall mental health.

In conclusion, managing stress and anxiety related to finances is an essential part of achieving financial wellness. By taking control of your finances, building an emergency fund, being mindful of your spending habits, seeking professional help, communicating with loved ones, and practicing self-care, you can reduce stress and anxiety related to finances and improve your overall mental health. Remember, managing financial stress takes time and effort, but it's a worthwhile investment in

Fostering a Healthy Relationship with Money

Fostering a Healthy Relationship with Money

Money is one of the most important aspects of our lives, and it's something we all have to deal with. However, many of us struggle with our relationship with money, and this can cause a lot of stress and anxiety. A healthy relationship with money is essential for financial stability, security, and long-term success. In this essay, we will explore the importance of a healthy relationship with money and provide some tips for fostering this kind of relationship.

One of the biggest reasons why a healthy relationship with money is so important is that it affects our mental health. Money-related stress and anxiety can cause a lot of problems in our lives. We may become less productive at work, have difficulty sleeping, and experience relationship problems. This is why it's important to develop a healthy relationship with money early on. By doing so, we can avoid many of the negative effects of financial stress and anxiety.

So, how can we foster a healthy relationship with money? The first step is to develop a clear understanding of our values and priorities. We need to ask ourselves what is truly important to us and what we want to achieve in life. This will help us create a clear financial plan and stick to it. For example, if we value experiences over material possessions, we may choose to save money for travel instead of buying a new car.

Another important aspect of fostering a healthy relationship with money is to develop a positive mindset. We need to start viewing money as a tool that can help us achieve our goals, rather than something that controls us. This means focusing on the opportunities that money can provide, such as the ability to travel, pursue higher education, or start a business. By viewing money in a positive light, we can reduce our stress and anxiety related to finances.

It's also important to develop good financial habits. This means creating a budget and sticking to it, avoiding unnecessary expenses, and saving for the future. When we have good financial habits, we are more likely to feel in control of our finances and less likely to experience stress and anxiety.

In addition to these steps, it's also important to educate ourselves about money. Many people have a limited understanding of personal finance, which can make it difficult to make informed decisions about our money. By taking the time to learn about budgeting, investing, and other financial topics, we can become more confident and in control of our financial situation.

Finally, it's important to remember that a healthy relationship with money is an ongoing process. We may experience setbacks and challenges along the way, but the key is to remain focused on our goals and continue to make progress. By continually evaluating our financial situation and making adjustments as necessary, we can achieve long-term financial success and security.

In conclusion, a healthy relationship with money is essential for financial stability, security, and long-term success. By developing a clear understanding of our values and priorities, adopting a positive mindset, developing good financial habits, educating ourselves about money, and remaining focused on our goals, we can foster a healthy relationship with money and avoid the negative effects of financial stress and anxiety.

Chapter Twenty-Six

Teaching Your Children About Money and Saving

Teaching children about money and saving is an important part of their financial education. By learning the value of money and how to manage it from a young age, children can develop healthy financial habits that will benefit them throughout their lives. In this essay, we will discuss some tips and strategies for teaching your children about money and saving.

Start early

It's never too early to start teaching your children about money. Even preschoolers can begin to understand the concept of money and its value. You can start by introducing them to coins and bills, and explaining what they are used for. You can also involve them in simple transactions like buying groceries or paying for a meal at a restaurant. By involving them in these everyday activities, you can help them understand the value of money and how it is used.

Set a good example

Children learn by example, so it's important to model good financial habits yourself. Show your children how to save money by setting a savings goal and working towards it. Let them see you making responsible financial decisions like paying bills on time, avoiding unnecessary expenses, and investing for the future. By setting a good example, you can help your children develop healthy financial habits.

Give them an allowance

Giving your children an allowance is a great way to teach them about money management. You can use the allowance as an opportunity to teach them about budgeting, saving, and spending wisely. For example, you could encourage them to save a portion of their allowance each week towards a specific goal, like buying a new toy or saving for a vacation. You can also use the allowance as an opportunity to teach them about the value of money by having them pay for some of their own expenses, like snacks or entertainment.

Teach them to budget

Budgeting is a key skill for managing money, and it's never too early to start teaching your children about it. You can teach them to budget by helping them create a spending plan for their allowance or other income. Help them identify their expenses, like toys, clothes, or entertainment, and encourage them to allocate their money accordingly. This will help them learn to prioritize their spending and make wise financial decisions.

Teach them to save

Saving is an important part of financial management, and it's important to teach children the value of saving from an early age. You can encourage them to save by setting savings goals, offering incentives for reaching those goals, and opening a savings account for them. Help them understand the benefits of saving, like earning interest on their money and having a safety net in case of unexpected expenses.

Teach them about investing

Investing is another important aspect of financial management, and it's never too early to introduce your children to the concept. You can teach them about investing by talking to them about stocks, bonds, and mutual funds. Explain how investing works and how it can help them grow their money over time. You can even involve them in your own investment decisions, like choosing stocks to invest in or tracking the performance of your portfolio.

Teach them to give back

Teaching your children about the importance of giving back can help them develop a sense of social responsibility and generosity. You can encourage them to donate a portion of their allowance to a charity or volunteer their time to a worthy cause. This will help them understand that money is not just about personal gain, but can also be used to make a positive impact on others.

In conclusion, teaching your children about money and saving is an important part of their financial education. By starting early, setting a good example, giving them an allowance, teaching them to budget and save, and introducing them to investing and giving back, you can help them develop healthy financial habits that will benefit them throughout their lives.

Age-Appropriate Money Lessons and Activities

Money is an essential part of our lives, and learning how to manage it is a critical skill that everyone needs to acquire. Teaching children about money and saving is an essential responsibility for parents to help them become financially savvy and independent adults. However, many parents often struggle with how to introduce the topic of money to their kids and what lessons to teach them at different stages of their development. In this essay, we will discuss age-appropriate money lessons and activities that parents can use to help their children learn about money and saving.

Preschoolers (Ages 3-5)

Preschoolers are at a stage where they are beginning to understand the concept of money and its value. At this age, children are not yet able to understand complex financial concepts, but it is a good time to start teaching them about basic money management. One of the most effective ways to introduce the concept of money to preschoolers is by using play money. Parents can use play money to teach their kids how to count and make simple transactions. Parents can also involve their kids in grocery shopping by asking them to help identify the cost of different items.

Elementary School (Ages 6-12)

As children grow older, they become more interested in money and its power. At this age, children have a better understanding of money, and parents can start teaching them more advanced money lessons. One of the best ways to teach kids about money management is through an allowance. Parents can give their children a weekly or monthly allowance and teach them how to save, spend, and donate their money. This is also a good age to introduce children to the concept of budgeting. Parents can help their children create a simple budget to track their expenses and savings.

Teenagers (Ages 13-18)

Teenagers are at an age where they are becoming more independent and are starting to make their financial decisions. At this age, parents can teach their children more complex financial concepts, such as credit, debt, and investment. Parents can help their children open a savings account and encourage them to save for long-term goals such as college or a car. Parents can also help their teenagers learn about credit and debt by explaining how credit cards work and how to avoid debt. This is also a good age to introduce children to the stock market and teach them about investing.

College Students and Young Adults

College students and young adults are at an age where they are starting their careers and making significant financial decisions. Parents can continue to provide guidance and support to their children at this stage by helping them make smart financial decisions. One of the best ways to help college students and young adults learn about money is by involving them in financial decision-making. Parents can help their children create a budget, understand the importance of saving for retirement, and teach them about the importance of having an emergency fund.

In conclusion, teaching children about money and saving is an essential responsibility for parents. By introducing age-appropriate money lessons and activities, parents can help their children become financially savvy and independent adults. Preschoolers can learn the basics of money management through play, while elementary school children can learn about budgeting and saving through an allowance. Teenagers can learn about more complex financial concepts such as credit, debt, and investment, and college students and young adults can continue to learn and make smart financial decisions with the guidance and support of their parents.

Encouraging Good Money Habits and Decision Making

Encouraging Good Money Habits and Decision Making

Teaching children good money habits and decision-making skills is essential for their future financial success. In today's world, where financial literacy is a necessity, parents and caregivers play a critical role in shaping children's attitudes towards money. It's important to start teaching children about money at a young age, as they are more receptive to learning and forming habits that will serve them well throughout their lives. In this essay, we will explore age-appropriate ways to encourage good money habits and decision-making skills.

Preschool Age (3-5 years old)

At this age, children are just beginning to understand the concept of money. Here are some simple ways to introduce money and savings to your child:

1. Start with the basics: Teach your child about the different coins and bills and their values. Let them play with coins and sort them by size or color.

2. Make saving fun: Give your child a piggy bank and encourage them to save coins. Set a goal for how much they should save, such as a toy or a treat they want. Celebrate their success when they reach their goal.

3. Use play to teach: Play store with your child using fake money and let them "buy" items from your "store." This will help them understand the concept of buying and selling.

4. Read books about money: There are many children's books that teach money concepts, such as "The Berenstain Bears' Trouble with Money" or "Alexander, Who Used to be Rich Last Sunday."

Elementary Age (6-11 years old)

At this age, children are more aware of the value of money and may receive an allowance or earn money through chores. Here are some ways to encourage good money habits:

5. Set a savings goal: Help your child set a savings goal, such as saving for a new bike or a video game. Encourage them to save a portion of their allowance or earnings each week towards their goal.

6. Teach them about budgeting: Help your child make a budget for their money. Show them how to allocate money for spending, saving, and giving.

7. Introduce the concept of interest: Teach your child about the concept of interest and how their savings can grow over time. Show them how to calculate simple interest on their savings.

8. Encourage entrepreneurship: Encourage your child to start a small business, such as a lemonade stand or a car wash. This will teach them about earning money, marketing, and managing expenses.

Teenagers (12-18 years old)

Teenagers are preparing for adulthood and will soon be managing their own finances. Here are some ways to encourage good money habits:

9. Open a bank account: Help your teenager open a checking and savings account. Teach them about the fees and interest rates associated with these accounts.

10. Teach them about credit: Teach your teenager about credit and the importance of building a good credit score. Show them how to use a credit card responsibly and pay off the balance in full each month.

11. Introduce investing: Teach your teenager about the basics of investing, such as stocks, bonds, and mutual funds. Show them how to research investments and diversify their portfolio.

12. Discuss financial responsibility: Have open and honest conversations with your teenager about the importance of financial responsibility. Discuss the consequences of overspending and the benefits of saving and investing.

In conclusion, teaching children good money habits and decision-making skills is crucial for their future financial success. By introducing money concepts at a young age and providing age-appropriate lessons, parents and caregivers can help children develop good money habits that will last a lifetime.

Preparing Your Children for Financial Independence

Preparing Your Children for Financial Independence

Financial independence is a goal that many parents hope their children will achieve. However, becoming financially independent requires more than just a good job and a high income. It also requires good money management skills and financial literacy. As a parent, it is important to start teaching your children about money and personal finance early on, so they can develop these skills and be prepared for their future. In this essay, we will explore some strategies for preparing your children for financial independence.

Start early

It is never too early to start teaching your children about money. As soon as they are old enough to understand the concept of money, you can start teaching them the value of saving and spending wisely. You can start by giving them an allowance and encouraging them to save a portion of it each week. This will help them develop good savings habits and learn the value of money.

Teach budgeting

Budgeting is an essential skill for financial independence. Teach your children how to create a budget and stick to it. This will help them learn to prioritize their spending and make responsible financial decisions. Encourage them to save a portion of their income each month and to track their expenses so they can see where their money is going.

Discuss debt

Debt is a reality of life for many people, but it is important to teach your children how to manage it responsibly. Talk to them about the dangers of credit card debt and how to avoid it. Teach them the importance of paying their bills on time and avoiding unnecessary debt. This will help them build good credit and avoid financial problems in the future.

Introduce investing

Investing is a powerful tool for building wealth over time. Introduce your children to the concept of investing and the different types of investments available. Teach them about the risks and rewards of investing and how to choose investments that are appropriate for their goals and risk tolerance. Encourage them to start investing early so they can take advantage of compounding returns.

Lead by example

One of the most effective ways to teach your children about money is to lead by example. Show them how you manage your finances and make responsible financial decisions. Let them see you saving for the future, avoiding debt, and investing for the long term. This will help them develop good financial habits and learn from your example.

Make it fun

Learning about money and personal finance doesn't have to be boring. Make it fun and engaging by playing games and doing activities that teach financial skills. For example, you can play a game where your children have to make financial decisions and manage their money in a simulated environment. This will help them learn important financial skills while having fun.

Teach entrepreneurship

Entrepreneurship is a great way to build wealth and achieve financial independence. Teach your children about entrepreneurship and how to start their own business. Encourage them to develop their skills and talents and find ways to monetize them. This will help them develop an entrepreneurial mindset and the skills they need to succeed in business.

Encourage education

Education is a key factor in achieving financial independence. Encourage your children to pursue their education and develop their skills. Help them explore different career options and find a path that will lead to financial success. Encourage them to continue learning throughout their lives and to invest in their own personal and professional development.

Be open and honest

Finally, it is important to be open and honest with your children about money. Don't hide financial problems or keep secrets about your finances. Instead, be transparent and honest about your financial situation and teach your children how to deal with financial challenges. This will help them develop the resilience and problem-solving skills they need to achieve financial independence.

Quick Tips:

Chapter Twenty-Seven

A Lifetime of Saving and Financial Success

- Start early: Teach your children about money and saving from a young age.
- Set a good example: Lead by example and demonstrate responsible money management.
- Give an allowance: Provide a regular allowance to teach children about budgeting and saving.
- Encourage saving: Encourage your children to save a portion of their allowance or earnings.
- Use a piggy bank: Use a piggy bank or jar to teach children about the importance of saving and seeing their savings grow.
- Set savings goals: Help your children set savings goals, such as saving for a toy or a special activity.
- Teach the value of money: Teach your children the value of money and how to make informed purchasing decisions.
- Use cash: Use cash instead of credit cards to help children understand the tangible value of money.
- Teach delayed gratification: Teach children the importance of waiting and saving for something they want instead of buying on

impulse.

- Teach budgeting: Teach children how to create and stick to a budget, including saving for future expenses.
- Teach about interest: Teach children about the concept of interest and how it can grow their savings over time.
- Open a savings account: Open a savings account for your child to help them learn about banking and interest.
- Teach about debt: Teach children about debt and the importance of avoiding unnecessary debt.
- Teach about credit: Teach children about credit and how to use it responsibly.
- Involve children in family finances: Involve your children in family financial decisions and discussions to help them understand the bigger picture.
- Play money games: Play fun money games with your children to help them learn about money management.
- Give financial gifts: Give financial gifts, such as savings bonds or stocks, to teach children about investing and the value of long-term savings.
- Take advantage of teachable moments: Use everyday situations, such as grocery shopping, to teach children about money management.
- Discuss needs vs. wants: Teach children the difference between needs and wants and how to prioritize spending.

- Teach about taxes: Teach children about taxes and how they impact their income and spending.
- Teach about insurance: Teach children about different types of insurance and the importance of protecting their finances.
- Teach about philanthropy: Teach children about giving back and the importance of philanthropy.
- Use online resources: Utilize online resources, such as financial education websites and apps, to help teach children about money management.
- Encourage entrepreneurial spirit: Encourage children to start their own small business or earn money through odd jobs to teach them about entrepreneurship and financial independence.
- Teach about the stock market: Teach children about the basics of the stock market and investing.
- Encourage saving for emergencies: Teach children the importance of saving for unexpected expenses or emergencies.
- Set a good credit example: Teach children the importance of building good credit and how to do so responsibly.
- Teach about retirement: Teach children about the importance of saving for retirement and starting early.
- Encourage charitable giving: Encourage children to donate a portion of their earnings to charity or a cause they care about.
- Reinforce good financial habits: Continually reinforce good financial habits and encourage children to continue to make smart

money decisions.

A lifetime of saving and financial success requires discipline, knowledge, and the ability to adapt to change. It is a journey that starts with small steps and grows over time with dedication and perseverance. This essay will explore the key principles of saving and financial success throughout different stages of life.

Starting Young

It is never too early to start saving money. Parents can teach children the value of money by encouraging them to earn their own money through chores or jobs. They can also encourage children to save a portion of their earnings and provide them with a piggy bank or savings account to store their money.

As children grow older, parents can introduce them to the basics of budgeting and money management. This can include teaching them about expenses and income, how to prioritize spending, and how to save for future goals.

Teenage Years

As teenagers enter the workforce, it is important to encourage them to save a portion of their earnings. Parents can also teach teenagers about credit and debt, including the importance of building a good credit score and avoiding high-interest debt.

College and Early Adulthood

College and early adulthood are critical times for financial success. This is when individuals start to establish their credit history and begin saving for future goals such as buying a home or starting a family.

One of the most important steps in achieving financial success during this time is establishing a budget. This includes tracking expenses and creating a plan to pay off any outstanding debt. It is also important to start building an emergency fund to cover unexpected expenses.

Building a Career

As individuals build their careers, they may face new financial challenges such as student loan repayment or saving for retirement. It is important to continue building an emergency fund and paying off debt while also prioritizing saving for retirement.

It is also important to explore different investment options such as employer-sponsored retirement plans or individual retirement accounts (IRAs). These investments can help individuals grow their savings and prepare for a financially secure retirement.

Mid-Life

As individuals enter their mid-life years, they may face new financial challenges such as caring for aging parents or saving for their children's education. It is important to continue building an emergency fund and contributing to retirement savings while also balancing these new financial obligations.

This is also a good time to reassess insurance needs such as life insurance, disability insurance, and long-term care insurance. These policies can help protect against unexpected expenses and ensure financial security for loved ones.

Retirement

Retirement is the ultimate goal of a lifetime of saving and financial success. This is when individuals can enjoy the fruits of their labor and the security of a well-planned financial future.

During retirement, it is important to continue managing expenses and adjusting spending to meet changing needs. It is also important to make sure that retirement savings last for the entirety of retirement by exploring different withdrawal strategies and investment options.

Conclusion

A lifetime of saving and financial success requires dedication, knowledge, and the ability to adapt to changing circumstances. It is a journey that starts in childhood and grows over time with discipline and perseverance. By following the key principles of saving and financial success throughout different stages of life, individuals can build a secure and financially stable future.

Celebrating Your Savings Milestones

Saving money is an important goal for many people. It can be challenging to stick to a budget and make regular contributions to your savings account, but the rewards are worth it. Celebrating your savings milestones can help keep you motivated and on track towards your financial goals.

There are many different milestones you can celebrate along your savings journey. The first and perhaps most important is simply getting started. Many people struggle to make that first contribution to their savings account, but once you've done it, you've taken a big step towards financial security. Celebrate this milestone by treating yourself to something small, like a nice meal or a new piece of clothing.

Another important milestone is reaching your first savings goal. Whether it's $1,000 or $10,000, achieving a savings goal takes discipline and hard work. Celebrate this milestone by taking a day off work or treating yourself to a weekend getaway.

As you continue to save, you may reach other important milestones, such as paying off a debt or reaching a certain level of net worth. These milestones can be celebrated in different ways depending on your personal preferences. You might choose to splurge on a big-ticket item like a new car or take a once-in-a-lifetime vacation.

It's important to remember that celebrating your savings milestones doesn't have to be expensive. There are many ways to mark these important moments without breaking the bank. For example, you might celebrate by cooking a special meal at home, hosting a game night with friends, or taking a day trip to a nearby park or beach.

One fun way to celebrate your savings milestones is to create a savings jar or chart. Every time you make a contribution to your savings account, add a colored bead or sticker to the jar or chart. When you reach a certain number of contributions or savings goals, treat yourself to a celebration.

It's also important to celebrate your progress even if you haven't yet reached a specific milestone. Every time you make a contribution to your savings account, you're taking a step towards financial security. Celebrate these small victories by treating yourself to something small, like a favorite treat or a relaxing evening at home.

Finally, don't forget to share your savings journey with others. By talking about your successes and challenges with family and friends, you can help inspire others to save and achieve their financial goals. You might also consider joining a savings group or online community where you can connect with others who are working towards similar goals.

In conclusion, celebrating your savings milestones is an important part of achieving financial success. By acknowledging your progress and treating yourself to small rewards along the way, you can stay motivated and on track towards your goals. Remember that saving money is a journey, not a destination, and enjoy the ride!

Adjusting Your Savings Strategies as Life Changes

Adjusting Your Savings Strategies as Life Changes

Saving money is an important part of maintaining financial stability and achieving long-term goals. However, as life changes, so do our financial needs and circumstances. This means that the savings strategies that worked in the past may not be effective for our current situation. In order to stay on track with our financial goals, it's important to regularly reassess our savings strategies and adjust them as needed. In this essay, we will discuss the importance of adjusting your savings strategies as life changes and provide some tips on how to do so effectively.

Why adjust your savings strategies?

Life is full of changes, and these changes can have a significant impact on our financial situation. Some of the most common life changes that can affect our savings strategies include getting married, having children, buying a home, changing jobs, and experiencing a financial setback. Each of these changes can have unique financial implications that require adjustments to our savings strategies.

For example, getting married can result in a change in household income and expenses, which can affect our ability to save. Having children can bring additional expenses such as childcare costs and medical bills, which may require a re-evaluation of our savings goals. Buying a home can increase our monthly expenses, including mortgage payments, property taxes, and maintenance costs, which can impact our ability to save for other goals. Changing jobs can result in a change in income or benefits, which can affect our savings strategies. Finally, experiencing a financial setback such as a job loss, illness, or unexpected expense can require us to reassess our savings priorities and goals.

The bottom line is that life is unpredictable, and our financial needs and circumstances are constantly changing. Adjusting our savings strategies is essential to ensuring that we stay on track with our financial goals and remain financially stable in the face of unexpected challenges.

Tips for adjusting your savings strategies

1. Reassess your goals: The first step in adjusting your savings strategies is to reassess your goals. Take some time to think about your current financial situation and your short-term and long-term goals. Are there any changes that need to be made to your savings goals? Do you need to prioritize different goals based on your current circumstances?

2. Evaluate your expenses: Once you have reassessed your goals, take a closer look at your expenses. Are there any areas where you can cut back or reduce expenses? For example, if you have recently bought a home, you may be able to reduce your entertainment or travel expenses to free up more money for mortgage payments and home maintenance costs.

3. Create a new budget: Based on your reassessment of your goals and expenses, create a new budget that reflects your current financial situation. Make sure to include your savings goals in your budget and adjust your savings rate as needed.

4. Explore new savings strategies: As your financial situation changes, you may need to explore new savings strategies. For example, if you have

recently changed jobs and your new employer offers a 401(k) plan, you may need to adjust your retirement savings strategy to take advantage of this new opportunity.

5. Automate your savings: One of the easiest ways to stay on track with your savings goals is to automate your savings. Set up automatic transfers from your checking account to your savings account or investment account to ensure that you are consistently saving a set amount each month.

6. Seek professional advice: If you are unsure how to adjust your savings strategies, consider seeking the advice of a financial professional. A financial planner can help you assess your financial situation, set new savings goals, and create a personalized savings plan.

Ensuring Your Financial Legacy

Planning for the future is crucial for a comfortable life. Saving money and investing it wisely can help you achieve your long-term financial goals. But what about your financial legacy? What kind of financial legacy do you want to leave behind for your loved ones? It is important to ensure your financial legacy, so that your family can continue to thrive even after you are gone.

One of the first steps to ensuring your financial legacy is to create a will. A will is a legal document that outlines how you want your assets to be distributed after you die. Without a will, your assets may be distributed according to the laws of the state, which may not align with your wishes. A will can also help minimize the chances of family disputes over inheritance.

In addition to a will, you may also want to consider setting up a trust. A trust is a legal arrangement in which a trustee holds and manages assets for the benefit of the beneficiaries. A trust can help ensure that your assets are distributed according to your wishes and can also provide certain tax benefits.

Another important step in ensuring your financial legacy is to review and update your beneficiary designations. Beneficiary designations are used to designate who will receive certain assets, such as life insurance policies or retirement accounts, after you die. It is important to ensure that your beneficiary designations are up to date and reflect your current wishes. Failure to update your beneficiary designations can lead to unintended consequences, such as leaving assets to an ex-spouse or an estranged family member.

In addition to these legal documents, it is also important to have open and honest conversations with your loved ones about your financial legacy. These conversations can help ensure that everyone is on the same page and understands your wishes. They can also help prevent misunderstandings and disputes after you are gone.

While planning for your financial legacy, it is also important to consider how you can make a positive impact on the world. Charitable giving is a great way to leave a legacy that goes beyond your family. By donating to charities and non-profit organizations, you can support causes that are important to you and make a difference in the lives of others.

There are many ways to give to charity, including direct donations, charitable gift annuities, and charitable trusts. These options can provide tax benefits and help ensure that your charitable giving is aligned with your overall financial plan.

In addition to charitable giving, you may also want to consider leaving a legacy through education. Investing in education can help ensure that future generations have the skills and knowledge they need to succeed. There are many ways to support education, including setting up a scholarship fund or making a donation to a university or college.

Another way to leave a positive financial legacy is to teach your children and grandchildren about financial responsibility. By instilling good money habits at a young age, you can help ensure that they are prepared to make smart financial decisions throughout their lives. Teaching them about budgeting, saving, and investing can help set them up for long-term financial success.

Finally, it is important to ensure that your financial legacy is aligned with your personal values and goals. What kind of legacy do you want to leave behind? What is important to you? By answering these questions and incorporating your values into your financial plan, you can create a legacy that reflects who you are and what you stand for.

In conclusion, ensuring your financial legacy is an important part of long-term financial planning. By creating a will, setting up a trust, reviewing beneficiary designations, having open conversations with loved ones, giving to charity, supporting education, teaching financial responsibility, and aligning your legacy with your values, you can leave a lasting impact on the world and your loved ones.

Chapter Twenty-Eight

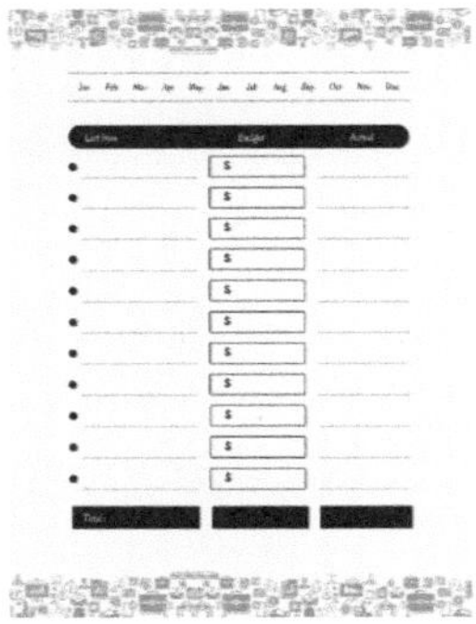

FINANCIAL GOAL
GIFT & DONATION

SD - #0027 - 140926 - C0 - 229/152/16 - PB - 9781776968800 - Matt Lamination